JELLY MONGERS

Glow-in-the-Dark Jelly

Titanic Jelly   Flaming Jelly

by the World's
Foremost Purveyors

BOMPAS & PARR

PHOTOGRAPHY BY CHRIS TERRY

Published in 2011 by Sterling Publishing Co., Inc.
387 Park Avenue South, New York, NY 10016

Text © Sam Bompas and Harry Parr, 2010
Design and layout © Anova Books, 2010

Photography © Chris Terry, 2010, except on pages: 10 Rogers Stirk Harbour + Partners/ 11, 160 Carl Palmer/12, 13, 16, 22–3 Greta Ilieva/14 Mark Dye/124–5 Charles Villyard/ 129, 152 Dan Price/150 Emma Rios/153 Barney Steel/9, 17, 93, 96, 123, 148, 149, 151 © Sam Bompas and Harry Parr

Illustrations: p.86 © Popperfoto/Getty Images/p.104, 160 © Emma Rios/pp.112–3 Hattie Newman/ p.119 © Illustrated London News Ltd/Mary Evans

Printed in China

Sterling ISBN: 978-1-4027-8480-4

For information about custom editions, special sales, premium and corporate purchases, please contact Sterling Special Sales Department at 800-805-5489 or specialsales@sterlingpublishing.com.

WHAT PEOPLE ARE SAYING ABOUT BOMPAS & PARR:

"Not since Heston Blumenthal burst on the scene has anyone brought such crazed ambition to food design." *THE TELEGRAPH*

"I think Bompas and Parr are geniuses. It's the principles of rock'n'roll applied to food." **ALEX JAMES, MUSICIAN AND COLUMNIST**

"Culinary deviants." *THE GUARDIAN*

"Like Gilbert and George, Bompas and Parr always seem to pop up together, often wearing cool oversized spectacles or ostentatiously fogeyish bow-ties." *THE TELEGRAPH*

"Willy Wonka during his freewheeling student days." *THE INDEPENDENT*

"England's leading jelly artists, or as they call themselves, jellymongers." *NEW YORK TIMES*

"If you're going to do silly, do it in style." *THE TIMES*

Named by *THE INDEPENDENT* as one of "the 15 people who will define the future of arts in Britain."

CONTENTS

INTRODUCTION

"When the going gets weird, the weird turn pro."

HUNTER S. THOMPSON

The life of a jellymonger is wobbly, largely ridiculous, and often downright weird. If it's not strange enough explaining to people what a *jellymonger* is, it's even stranger describing what else we do with food and how we really do make a living selling jelly.

The jelly business started when we tried to set up a stall at Borough Market in London in the summer of 2007. They weren't interested but we managed to pull in a couple of jobs making fresh fruit jellies for parties. No one was making jello, so there was an obvious gap in the market. Our inspiration came from two sources: childhood nostalgia and the knowledge that England used to be famous in the culinary world for two things — jelly and roasting. Jelly had somehow taken a serious tumble in the nation's affections. After the *Sunday Times* included us in an article about the renaissance of traditional English food, business took off dramatically.

If you think that jelly starts and ends with the lurid stuff you get at children's parties, then you've got a lot to learn. Jelly has a long, illustrious history. We didn't know what we were getting ourselves into until we started studying old cookbooks. Jelly used to be one of the noblest things you could eat at a meal. Forget making jelly with champagne: jelly used to be made with gold. Even Henry VIII was a fan, requesting it to grace his banqueting tables on state occasions. Victorian England was jelly's heyday: embarrassed French chefs even came on secret pilgrimages across the channel to get jelly tips and pick up exquisite molds.

We are working hard to restore jelly to its culinary throne. With this book, we've been given the opportunity to tell you everything we know about it. The best thing about jelly is that, with decent instructions, it's really easy to make and the results are spectacular. Jelly is magical: it has the ability to make people laugh hysterically, is loaded with nostalgia, and best of all, can taste wild. OK, we're not giving a sermon here, but you get the idea: jelly rocks.

When you start making and serving proper jelly, we hope that your views on food will change. People love jelly. It's one of the only foods to be guaranteed a

Our first jelly commission – the Innocent village fête in 2007.

reaction of some sort. The reaction we get has made us reassess what food is really about. Jelly generates so much excitement that we wondered how we could approach other types of food to elicit similar reactions.

Bompas & Parr has always been about creating culinary projects that explode people's preconceived notions of food. Whether it's assaulting people's senses with scratch 'n' sniff cards at food movies or creating walk-in clouds of gin and tonic, we've found there's no limit to what you can do with food. The same is true for jelly. By the time you've finished reading this book, you'll see that there's a whole lot more to jelly than you may have thought. And I'll bet we'll still be coming up with new things to do with jelly many years from now.

Neither of us trained to be chefs. The weird thing is, Sam would probably be a politician by now if he hadn't got into jelly whereas Harry trained for six years to become an architect but left it all for jelly. Bizarrely it was Harry's professor who suggested that there was a lot of mileage in jelly (maybe he was trying to say something about Harry's architectural prowess). So, with no formal culinary training, our approach to cooking is vastly different to most people's in the food industry.

As the business progressed, we really needed to get a grip on making our own molds. Those beautiful copper Victorian molds are extortionately expensive, and

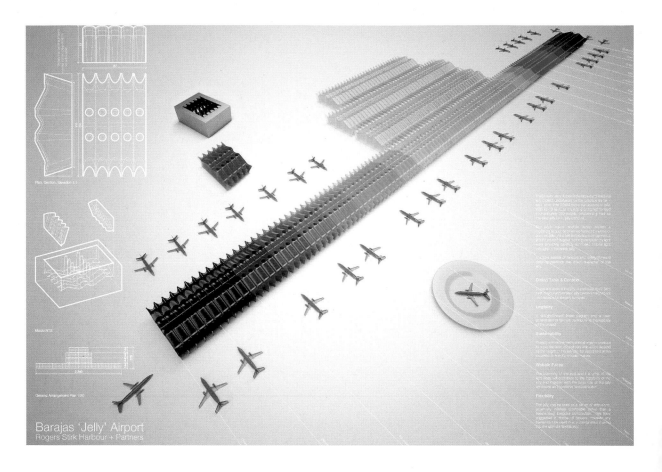

Barajas 'Jelly' Airport
Rogers Stirk Harbour + Partners

with no molds we didn't have a hope of doing anything decent with jelly. So, never shy of a challenge, we gave ourselves a huge headache. We invited architects to design jellies in the shape of their buildings and offered to make the molds for them. We called it the Architectural Jelly Design Competition and we did it to benefit disaster relief charity Article 25. We then planned a jelly banquet, to be held in the stunning portico of University College London. We were all set to kickstart a jelly comeback.

The jelly banquet became one of 2008's stories of the summer (see also p.150). It was big news. Everyone was going jelly crazy. It was helped by securing the support of some of the biggest names in architecture, including Lord Foster and Rogers Stirk Harbour + Partners. Foster designed a jelly in homage to his "wobbly" millennium bridge, and Rogers created the genius Barajas "jelly" airport — a striking multiflavored modular jelly. Sam even ended up taking jellies on BBC Radio 4's "Today" program.

The impending banquet forced us to work out how to make jelly molds. Using the same programs that architects use to design buildings, we're able to model the jelly and then translate it to a physical model, using a process called 3D printing. The 3D printer prints glue onto a moving bed of plaster, allowing a model of the jelly to be created. The resulting form can then be vacuum-formed with plastic to create a functional mold. Of course, it's not as simple as it sounds and we are still perfecting the technique.

We had more than 100 entries into the competition and we assembled a panel of design and food experts to judge them in terms of innovation, esthetics, and, most importantly, "wobble-factor." Professor Stephen Gage, from University College London and one of the judges of the competition, summed up the architectural appeal of jelly like this:

> *"As babies, we first learn about our world by touching it and putting bits of it in our mouth. Part of our subconscious appreciation of shape may well be a dim memory of how it might feel in our mouth. Thus a dome is round and cooly satisfying, while a pointed building is like a sharp and dangerous knife. Jelly architecture returns architecture to the mouth, where we can once again taste it."*

Above and Opposite
Entries from the Architectural Jelly Design Competition. Above left: *Wobbly Bridge* by Lord Foster; Above right: *Wheatgrass Jelly* by Atkins Global; Opposite: *Barajas Jelly Airport* by Rogers Stirk Harbour + Partners.

Well, that's enough theory for now. We had more than 2,000 people due to attend the banquet, and we knew that we would have to do something extraordinary to keep them all entertained. Although jellies are striking, it's hard to make them very big. So for the jellies we made a 46-foot long table, which held hundreds of individually illuminated jellies, and was driven by an ingenious "waggle engine" that made everything wobble. To set it all off, we commissioned a jelly ballet to be performed on the steps of the portico. Harry made giant plastic spoons for the dancers to use to interpret the music.

The night really started to get under way when Heston Blumenthal, who had been at the banquet getting inspiration for his own TV series "Feast," agreed to hand out the prize to the winning architect. At this point, the crowd started shouting "fight, fight, fight," drowning him out until two brave pioneers dived into a pool full of jelly and started wrestling. It was a great jelly moment.

Later in the evening, as the clock struck 11p.m., a jelly in the shape of St. Paul's Cathedral was hurled out of the portico and onto the crowd below. Within seconds, a huge food fight broke out. It was something that we weren't expecting, but it was definitely fun.

Opposite: *Jelly St Paul's Cathedral*, designed by Bompas & Parr.
Above: Harry and Sam at Alcoholic Architecture, their gin cloud installation.

Jelly and alcohol go hand in hand. Those jellies that Henry VIII served were alcoholic, and throughout history alcohol has often been added to jelly. To see how far we could really push alcohol consumption, we created Alcoholic Architecture, a bar where people could literally walk into a cloud of vaporized gin and tonic. The alcoholic fog was a global hit, although we suspect that it will be outlawed if we ever try to repeat it: some things are best left as memories (see also p.152).

More child-friendly was working with Jell-O®, who gave us the opportunity to build some wonderfully ambitious jelly sculptures. We even created a vast jelly map of America for an edition of the "Early Show" on CBS. Although it took months of work to design and make the molds, the hardest part was getting up at 3 a.m. to unmold all the individual jellies that made up the map.

Our approach to food has been influenced heavily by creating culinary events and then observing how people react to what's around them. Food is a really complicated subject. We have to eat to survive, yet what we put in our mouths is loaded with so much meaning that it's easy to forget this. Sure, we both like good food, but good food comes in many forms: a bag of cheeseburger-flavored potato chips is just as incredible as anything that you would eat at a Michelin-starred restaurant. And with jelly, high and low cultures really do get slammed together. For example, the technology we use to design and make jelly molds is of the moment, yet that same mold can be filled with organic fruit or with artificially flavored jelly from a box. The truth is that by the time you unmold and present the jelly, the original ingredients are only a very small part of people's experience.

Food should be, above all else, enjoyable. Next time you're invited to a dinner party, don't bring trendy bijou chocolates. Instead bring ordinary foil-wrapped chocolates — but arrange them on a silver tray in a pyramid. It's cheaper, more fun, and unless you're a chocolate fascist, probably as tasty. It's all too easy to have food prejudice, but it is worth thinking for a moment about why things are as they are. For example, don't forget that there are far more chemicals in the kitchen of El Bulli than there are in any burger.

In a world where food is becoming so worthy, it's time to rediscover the joy that can come from cooking. Jelly is as good a place as any to start enjoying food. So, whether you make jelly with foraged fruit or with juice from the supermarket, you're still going to have fun. And fun should, for once, be important.

The wobble that woos: jellying in America.

A BRIEF HISTORY OF JELLY

Jelly has quite some history. It's been around in one form or another for thousands of years. The origins of jelly are somewhat shrouded in mystery, though one thing is clear: if you boil any meat or fish and let the stock cool, then guess what, you've got jelly. OK, so it's more like pork pie jelly than raspberry jelly but, like it or not, the basis of both is the same. And hundreds of years ago people realized that the jelly they could make from boiling meat had a lot of potential.

Out of curiosity, we decided that we needed to get medieval and make jelly from scratch; there's no point calling yourself a jellymonger if you can't take flesh and turn it into dessert. We found that by taking a pig's worth of feet and boiling them up, you can indeed make a passable jelly. As long as you don't eat it that is, because the downside is that it tastes pretty porkie. If Jell-O® sold pig-flavored jello, we don't imagine it would fly off the shelves — although we do admire Marks and Spencer for Percy Pig; a gelatin-based candy shaped like a friendly pig is warped genius.

Unsuprisingly, some of the earliest known jelly recipes were for savory jellies. Take Taillevant, head cook to Charles V, who in 1381 gave a recipe for a "jelly of slimy fish, and of meat." Sounds disgusting, but apparently it turned out OK. And, even then, clarity and a clean flavor were important to jellies: not many recipes include the line "If you wish to make jello, you do not need to sleep." Making a decent jelly involved lots of clarifying of the stock using egg whites, and lots of straining through expensive jelly cloths. Making jelly took time. And time means money — so serving a jelly was an impressive, and generous, act. When the soon-to-be King Henry IV was traveling back from a pilgrimage to the Holy Lands in 1393, he authorized his cook to travel to Venice to buy three yards of fabric for making jelly cloths. That's some jelly emergency he was having.

In medieval Britain, it wasn't unusual to have sweet and savory flavors combined — sugar was rare and so it was used like a spice and added to almost anything. Take mincemeat tarts; they were traditionally meat-based, containing more ground mutton than the usual bits and pieces. And, by the way, they taste amazing — the meat loosens the texture, making them much lighter.

Sam and Harry get Victorian with their meaty desserts.

So perhaps jelly did always taste a little meaty and people were just used to it.

In the late medieval period, fasting was the name of the game. For many days in the Church calendar, fish had to be eaten instead of meat. Forty consecutive days eating fish during Lent was enough to deaden everyone's palates. For the poor, Lent meant 40 days of salted fish. And for the rich few, jelly provided the variety and amusement. It's at this point that the records start to refer to jelly molds. Fish-shaped jellies made with sweet almond milk were popular, as was the strange practice of making replica jelly eggs.

By the sixteenth century, jelly was becoming more refined as a dish in its own right. Cooks had discovered that a variety of gelling agents could be used for setting jelly. These included calves feet and the curious isinglass, which is made from the swim bladders of sturgeon. The addition of sugar produced a jelly that was more recognizable to the modern palate. Jelly was the preserve of the rich and was used liberally as a form of conspicuous consumption. At this time, sugar was wildly expensive, and kept under lock and key by the mistress of the house. Making sweetened jelly was an easy way to demonstrate wealth.

Color too became a priority. We were relieved to see that old recipes often suggest making striped jelly by making a batch of jelly and then splitting it into parts and coloring them differently. Often, when we are making jellies that are going to be used for photoshoots, this is exactly what we do. Cooks once used almond milk to turn jellies white; we just use milk. And forget using saffron to turn a jelly yellow. At this point, the cook's art lay in making something that looked like a jelly rather than making something that we would call authentic. A red jelly did not signify that it would taste of strawberries.

The separation of savory and sweet was made complete by the development of the banquet. We think of a "banquet" as a feast, but the term was originally used to describe the new course that developed during the Renaissance: a sweet final course, served to round off the meal. In England, this course even had its own architecture: the banqueting house. These were ornate structures built solely for creating a showcase for sugary desserts. It's no surprise to learn that Harry is particularly keen on building one.

One important dish on the banquet table was *leche*: a sweet milk jelly perfumed with rosewater. The jelly was cut into squares and one half was gilded to create an impressive checkerboard effect. This combination of jelly and gold laid the foundations for the elaborate suspensions of gold leaf in Victorian jellies. For Sam, it has also laid the foundations of an extremely expensive addiction.

Early banqueting tables had elaborate sugar sculptures and molded marzipan pastes, formed into interesting shapes using hand-carved wooden molds. It wasn't long before a whole industry developed around making molds. The first jelly molds were carved from sycamore wood and were used to make flummery (a sweet fruit pudding), which evolved into the modern blancmange (a sweet milky pudding-like dessert). A century later, complex copper molds allowed cooks to experiment with such culinary witticisms as full-color replicas of bacon and eggs.

The golden age of jelly dawned at the start of the eighteenth century. Jelly-glasses were developed to show off multicolored jellies in their full splendor, and from the mid-eighteenth century the Staffordshire potteries began producing some of the earliest ceramic molds, made from salt-glazed stoneware. These molds are suprisingly shallow and incredibly fragile. Food historian Ivan Day kindly showed us how to use them – although it was somewhat nerve-racking. We made blancmange fish and then gilded them.

Ivan also showed us a very rare obelisk creamware mold made by Neale and Son in about 1790. These molds are incredible – they were specifically developed to make jellies for decoration rather than eating. The mold comes in two parts: an outer shell and an ornately decorated internal core with a base. You pour jelly into the gap between the outer mold and the core. Then you remove the outer mold leaving a thin layer of jelly covering the decorated core. The idea is that the gentle scalloped edges of the jelly would catch the flickering candlelight and animate the fauna painted on the core. Ivan had only recently bought one of these molds at vast expense and he was keen to give it a try, especially because every other example was in a museum case. In practice, these molds are really hard to use but they illustrate that jelly really did signify good taste.

The fashion for jellies was a boomtime for the more adventurous entrepreneur. We like to think that we coined the word jellymonger, but in eighteenth-century Manchester, Elizabeth Raffald was making money selling, among other things, "Globe Jellies." The concept was simple – using a large bowl, clear jellies could be set to make a huge convex lens. Her innovations, however, were anything but simple. She suggested fanciful creations of clear fish-ponds with white or gold fish (made from flummery) set on the bottom; the contents of whole fruitbaskets arranged in jelly; and a jelly planetarium of milky-white flummery moons and stars set against a black night sky.

Then came the Victorian era, when jelly reached its pinnacle. Copper molds were more complex than ever, and had the advantage of being excellent conductors, allowing the jelly to be removed easily with just a dip in warm water. Hollow inserts were developed for molds, such as the Alexandra Cross. A cross-shaped insert was placed inside the main body of red jelly as it set. When solid, the insert was filled with warm water, then unmolded, and the cavity filled with a white jelly. Presented and cut horizontally, the jelly emerged as slices bearing the Danish flag. They even had special knives for cutting jellies.

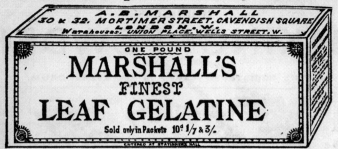
Advertisement for our hero Mrs. Marshall's line of gelatin.

MOULDS FOR HOT & COLD ENTRÉES & SAVOURIES.

No. 215B.
BUTTERFLY MOULD.
4s. 6d. per doz.

No. 215C.
FANCY MOULD.
Copper tinned,
8s. per doz.

No. 215D.
FANCY MOULD.
Copper tinned,
8s. per doz.

No. 215E.
FANCY MOULD.
Copper tinned,
8s. per doz.

No. 215F.
FANCY MOULD.
Copper tinned,
8s. per doz.

No. 215G.
FANCY MOULD.
Copper tinned,
8s. per doz.

No. 215H.—COPPER BOMBE.
9s. per doz.

No. 217.—FLUTED FLEUR RING.
1s. each. Plain Fleur Rings, 6d. & 9d. each.

No. 209.—2s. per doz.

No. 215I.
WALNUT MOULDS.
For Petits Fours, etc., 1s. 6d. per doz.

SPECIMEN PAGE FROM 'BOOK OF MOULDS.'

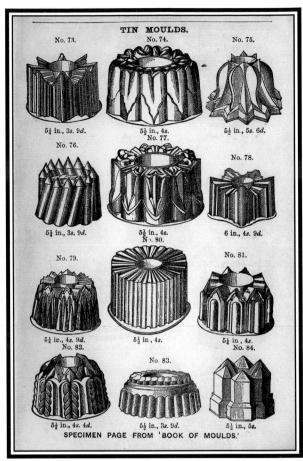

TIN MOULDS.

No. 73.
5¼ in., 3s. 9d.

No. 74.
5½ in., 4s.

No. 75.
5½ in., 5s. 6d.

No. 76.
5¼ in., 3s. 9d.

No. 77.
5¼ in., 4s.

No. 78.
6 in., 4s. 9d.

No. 79.
5¼ in., 4s. 9d.

No. 80.
5½ in., 4s.

No. 81.
5¼ in., 4s.

No. 82.
5½ in., 4s. 4d.

No. 83.
5½ in., 3s. 9d.

No. 84.
5½ in., 5s.

SPECIMEN PAGE FROM 'BOOK OF MOULDS.'

Mrs. Marshall showcases her own-brand molds.

Pages 22–23: A spread for a single diner at the Victorian Breakfast we created at Warwick castle. For full details see p.149.

Mrs. Marshall, owner of Marshall's Cookery School, combined a fine line in jellies with an even finer line in marketing. Her books are exercises in self-promotion; recipes for Alexandra jelly are shamelessly supplemented by a catalog of her own brand of molds. And she insisted that her readers use her own brand of leaf gelatin; her advertisements warn against the lesser-quality imitations of her competitors. This allows us to suggest that going to www.jellymongers.co.uk is a great place to start any mold collection.

The widespread popularity of jelly, combined with advances in food processing technology, led to the first preparations of so-called "table jellies" by companies such as Rowntree's and Hartley's in the U.K. In 1881, Rowntree's started the first domestic production of fruit pastilles, which had previously been the preserve of the French. This success, coupled with some studious forays into artificial flavoring and gelling, led to the production of Rowntree's Table Jellies in 1901.

The story of Rowntree's and Hartley's is remarkably similar: two companies headed by entrepreneurial grocers, which rose to dominate the market. The Hartley's factory at Aintree (just north of Liverpool) was the center of a village dedicated to producing jams and jellies. Each year, the town's residents stopped other work to pick a bumper crop of fruit, which was then transformed into "jelly cubes." The easily recognizable jelly cube is unique to the U.K. – the rest of Europe and the United States use powdered gelatin.

Powdered gelatin was first patented in the United States in 1845, but was not widely used. Then, at the beginning of the twentieth century, fruit syrups were added to the gelatin, and a product called Jell-O® was born. It soon became a must-have dessert on every table. Recently, we were commisioned by Jell-O® to create a whole series of molds for a media tour of the U.S. It was a lot of fun, even if we weren't allowed to sell directly to kids (unlike Bill Cosby, the face of Jell-O® for decades).

By the 1950s, jelly became more popular then ever; jelly is quick to make, and the new refrigerators meant that setting times were drastically reduced. Furthermore, jelly had come to be seen as a healthy alternative dessert, so much so that in the 1950s *Vogue* published an article on the newest fad for the jelly diet, pitting one wobble against another.

As jelly became increasingly easy and cheap to make, it led to a rapid decline in the craft of making jelly molds. By the start of World War II, the jelly-mold industry in England had effectively ceased. Plastic molds helped to replace part of the void that was left, but the figurative designs hardly reflect jelly's fine pedigree.

At Bompas and Parr we're changing all that. We've made molds of everything, from nuclear submarines to skyscrapers. Making our own molds allows us to explore jello's heritage and to push the boundaries of the medium. And we're not the only ones who have rediscovered jelly. Innovative chefs are constantly delivering new flavors and textures. Jelly has endless possibilities.

THE UNIVERSAL
JELLY PRINCIPLE

If stable food is not your thing, you should be pleased to hear that almost anything can be turned into a jelly. With a distinctly misguided spirit of adventure, we once created an entire Christmas dinner in one tall and very wobbly striped jelly. There were layers of Brussels sprouts, parsnips, potatoes, stuffing, bread sauce, and of course, turkey consommé studded with artfully positioned mini-sausages and strips of bacon. Once you can master this jelly Everest — it had jelly foothills made of champagne, burgundy, port, and sherry — you're qualified to jelly anything. At least, we like to think so.

To make a jelly, whether it's sweet or savory, you need to combine two components: a liquid and gelatin. At its most basic, the jelly recipe can be turned into a sum:

$$Liquid + Gelling\ Agent = Jelly$$

This principle will be expanded upon and explained in the next section. And by the time you are done reading it, you will be able to turn any liquid into a jelly.

Turn the page for a step-by-step guide to basic jelly making.

STEP ONE: CHOOSE YOUR MOLD

First fill your mold with water and pour this water into a measuring cup. Knowing the volume of liquid that you need to fill your mold allows you to calculate your gelatin. To get you started, here's a good rule of thumb:

1 leaf (sheet) of gelatin sets ½ cup of liquid

How simple is that? If you are setting the jelly in a glass and not planning on ummolding it, use less gelatin — see the table for guidance. Use either platinum or gold leaf gelatin: it's available online at www.oetkeronline.co.uk. Using scissors, cut up each leaf of gelatin into about 6 pieces and put them in a heatproof bowl. Use a measuring cup to mix up the required volume of liquid. This could be anything — fruit juice, wine, even cola. Next, pour some of this liquid over the gelatin so it is just covered. Leave for at least 10 minutes, or until the gelatin has softened.

Powdered gelatin is harder to use and the results are not as good. It tends to be available as ¼ oz sachets. If you don't intend to unmold your jelly, use 1 sachet of powdered gelatin per 2 cups of liquid. If you do intend to unmold your jelly, use 1½ sachets per 2 cups of liquid. If you can't get ahold of leaf gelatin, use this conversion as a guide in all the recipes in this book and make your quantities up to 2 cups, not 2 generous cups. (See p.145 for the alternative method for melting.)

Mold volume	Unmolding jelly	Not unmolding jelly
1¼ cups	3 leaves gelatin	2.2 leaves gelatin
1¾ cups	4	2.9
generous 2 cups	5	3.6
2½ cups	6	4.3
3 cups	7	5
generous 3 cups	8	5.7
3½ cups	9	6.4
4 cups	10	7.1

STEP TWO:
MELTING THE GELATIN

Put some hot water in a small saucepan and bring it up to a slow simmer. Then place the bowl of softened gelatin on top. Stir from time to time until the gelatin has dissolved. This should take about 10 minutes, but it can take longer if you are using milk as the liquid.

STEP THREE:
COMBINING THE GELATIN
WITH THE MIXTURE

Add the remaining liquid to the bowl of melted gelatin and give it a good stir. Then pour the contents of the bowl through a sieve and back into the measuring cup. The sieve will catch any small lumps of undissolved gelatin, and if you are using lemon juice it will catch the seeds.

Now slowly pour the unset jelly into your mold. If there are any air bubbles on the surface, skim them off using a teaspoon. Otherwise, they will still be there when the jelly has set. Place the jelly in the refrigerator, and about six hours later it will be set and ready for unmolding.

STEP FOUR:
UNMOLDING

Jelly comes to life when it is unmolded. The unmolding process is theoretically straightforward. Put the jelly mold into a basin of warm water until a little of the jelly around the edge has melted and then turn it out onto a plate.

It sounds easy, but there's real skill in judging the time the mold needs to be submerged in the warm water. Sometimes you must be patient; on other occasions, it will unmold in a flash. Depending on the thickness of the metal or plastic and the temperature of the water, it can take between two seconds and 30 seconds for the jelly to release.

When you unmold directly onto a plate, the jelly will stick to the surface wherever it lands. To prevent this, wet the plate before turning out the jelly. This allows you to reposition the jelly to the plate's center. If you've got this far, you're almost a jelly pro. Good work! If you are serving jelly for a dinner party, you can unmold it in advance and leave it on its plate in the refrigerator, where it will keep quite happily for several hours.

SUGAR SYRUP

Jelly straight from the refrigerator will be thoroughly chilled. Remember that the flavor of anything cold is less obvious than something at room temperature. So when making jelly, the liquid you use must be slightly sweeter than you want it finally to taste.

The best way of adding sugar to a juice is to use sugar syrup (also known as simple syrup), which dilutes and sweetens the fruit juice at the same time. It's a good idea to dilute fruit juice down before making it into a jelly, otherwise, it will be more like jam.

If you want total control over the sweetness of any jelly in this book, use sugar syrup and omit any other sugar from the recipe. And use a combination of syrup and water to make up the volume of the fruit juice you're using.

Making sugar syrup is very easy and if you have some leftover, it's got plenty of other uses. It's the best way to get sweetness into cocktails. By the same token it's handy for making iced coffee in the summer. You can also use the syrup as the base for poaching fruit and adding sweetness to fruit salads.

Bring the water to a boil in a saucepan and take it off the heat. Then stir in the sugar until it has dissolved. Easy!

MAKES ABOUT 1⅓ PINTS

GENEROUS 2 CUPS WATER

2½ CUPS SUPERFINE OR GRANULATED SUGAR

Of course, if you don't think you will need this much syrup just adjust the volume of water and weight of sugar proportionately at a ratio of about 1:1 (equal parts water and sugar).

If you have leftover syrup, it can be stored covered in the refrigerator for up to two weeks.

Frequently asked
Questions:

What type of gelatin should I use and why?

Always use leaf gelatin. Leaf gelatin creates jelly with the smoothest texture and is cleaner tasting than powdered gelatin. Gelatin is graded Olympic medal style — but jelly is more fun than sports, so there is also a top-notch platinum grade. Use either platinum or gold grade: anything else will be less than satisfactory. Luckily, most supermarkets will take your money in return for a pack of their finest gold or platinum grades. The higher up the medal table your gelatin is, the purer it will be, with corresponding improvements in clarity, taste, and gelling strength.

But the package says I should use a specific amount of gelatin.

This is where the dark art of jellying comes in. Don't be fooled by what it says on the back of the packaging. If you're going to unmold your jelly (and you really should), you need to use more than it says. A good amount to use is 1 leaf for every scant ½ cup of liquid. This way, it will be easier to handle when you unmold it. A lesser amount — say, $7/10$ of a leaf per scant ½ cup — will create a jelly that will have little structural integrity for unmolding but will be very tender (use this only for jelly set in glasses). Of course, the amount of gelatin required also depends on the proportions of the mold that you are using and the ingredients of the jelly: acid makes for a weaker gel; alcohol can strengthen a gel up to a point; and sugar makes a stronger gel too. (You'll find more information on gel strengths in the section Gelling Agents, p.144–146.) If in doubt, always err on the side of caution. It's better that your jelly is gracing your table, albeit a little firm, rather than relegated to the bottom of your sink.

What kind of mold should I use?

When starting off, a tinned copper mold is ideal. If you haven't yet hit it big time and commissioned a custom-made one of your pet polar bear, don't worry. Old American aluminum molds are good to use; in general, anything metal is a hot bet — although using a saucepan is perhaps a bit silly.

If you're out of metal molds, go for plastic. You can use any plastic container or even the plastic molds that supermarket foods come in. Now is not the time to dust down your granny's glass and ceramic mold collection. The impending disaster will put you off jellying for years. Later in the book, we'll explain how you can get your glass and ceramic molds back into active service, but until then you'll have to be patient.

Can I make it set faster?

Yes. If you're short of time, stir the jelly mixture in a bowl set over another bowl half-filled with ice and water. If you're really in a hurry, add a handful of salt to the iced water. Your jelly will start to set in minutes, but don't forget to stir: freezing destroys jelly. When the jelly starts to thicken and becomes slightly, but not too, lumpy, it can be poured into a mold. It will still take about two hours in the refrigerator to set firmly enough to be unmolded. If you do need to get a jelly to set in a hurry, you can always add some extra gelatin. This will help it gel quicker, but if you don't eat it quickly it will get significantly firmer the longer it stays in the refrigerator.

EASY FRUIT JELLIES

ORANGE JELLY

This tasty jelly blows children's party jelly out of the water. It's a great place to start exploring real jelly and it shows just how simple a fresh fruit jelly is to make.

FOR GENEROUS 2 CUPS, SERVES 4

JUICE FROM ABOUT 4 MEDIUM ORANGES (TO MAKE 1¼ CUPS)

JUICE OF ½ LEMON

SCANT ½ CUP SUGAR SYRUP

SCANT ½ CUP WATER

5 LEAVES OF GELATIN

First the fun part – choose your mold! Use water and a measuring cup to check its volume. Then adjust the recipe as necessary. If you are going to fill glasses with the jelly, get these ready. Regardless of whether you are using a mold or glasses, it's a good idea to get into a habit of putting them on a tray to catch any accidental spills as you move the jelly to the refrigerator.

Cut the oranges in half and squeeze them, seeds and all, into a large measuring cup. Keep going until you have 1¼ cups. Then squeeze in the lemon juice.

The orange juice is going to be relatively tart, so you will need to sweeten it. Add about equal quantities of syrup and water to the orange juice until you reach 2 generous cups. If you think that you have exceptionally sweet oranges, then by all means add less syrup. In any case, the volume of the liquid must reach 2 generous cups.

Now for turning it into a jelly. Cut the leaves of gelatin into a few pieces and place in a heatproof bowl. Add a few tablespoons of the juice mixture so that the gelatin is just covered. Let the gelatin soften for 10 minutes while you bring a small pan of water to a simmer.

Place the bowl of softened gelatin over the simmering water and stir from time to time until totally melted. This will take about 10 minutes. Pour the remainder of the juice mixture over the melted gelatin and stir to combine.

Finally, pour through a sieve into a large measuring cup and then carefully fill your mold. Refrigerate until set.

Easy lemon jelly

Freshly made lemon jelly is utterly delicious. But if you use lemon juice, you will run into a couple of problems. The first is that it is a pale color; the second is that if you use too much lemon juice, there's a danger that its acidity will stop the gelatin from doing its work. One way of getting a lovely yellow color is by infusing lemon zest in sugar syrup; even simpler is to add a little bit of orange juice, which turns the jelly a radiant lemon yellow. This recipe is particularly good for children's palates — if you want something more grown-up, then make the tart Lemonade Jelly (p.39).

FOR GENEROUS 2 CUPS, SERVES 4

½ CUP LEMON JUICE

SCANT ½ CUP ORANGE JUICE

½ CUP SUGAR SYRUP

⅔ CUP WATER

5 LEAVES OF GELATIN

Squeeze the juices into a large measuring cup. Then add the sugar syrup and water.

Cut the leaves of gelatin into a few pieces and place in a heatproof bowl. Add a few tablespoons of the juice mixture so that the gelatin is just covered. Let the gelatin soften for 10 minutes while you bring a small pan of water to a simmer.

Place the bowl of softened gelatin over the simmering water and stir from time to time until totally melted. This takes about 10 minutes. Then pour the remainder of the juice mixture over the melted gelatin and stir to combine. Pour through a sieve into a large measuring cup and then carefully fill your mold. Refrigerate until set.

LEMONADE JELLY

Here's a fun recipe for making a really zingy lemon jelly. This is one that works best when it has an ultrasoft set, so it is best to set it in four wine glasses. The egg whites may seem strange, but they give it an incredible fizz.

First zest and juice the lemons, then put everything into a small saucepan along with the sugar and water. Heat almost to a simmer so the sugar dissolves and the zest colors the liquid. Keep on a very low heat for an additional 5 minutes, then strain the liquid through a sieve into a large measuring cup to remove any seeds and the zest. Add additional cold water until you reach a generous 2 cups.

Cut up 4 leaves of gelatin into a heatproof bowl and pour over a little of the lemon mixture. When the gelatin is soft, melt it over a pan of simmering water. Then add the rest of the lemon mixture and pour everything through a sieve into a clean bowl.

Put the egg whites into a bowl and then pour over the jelly mixture. Set this bowl over a larger bowl filled with ice water and whisk, using a hand-held electric mixer, until the mixture has a good head of froth at the top and is just beginning to set. Don't go too far, or it will turn into a lemon mousse!

When the mixture feels cool to the touch, pour it into the four glasses. Obviously, this is a recipe where you don't need to skim the jelly before it sets.

GENEROUS 2 CUPS, SERVES 4

ZEST AND JUICE OF 3 LEMONS

SCANT ½ CUP SUPERFINE SUGAR

SCANT ½ CUP WATER, PLUS EXTRA AS NECESSARY

4 LEAVES OF GELATIN

3 LARGE EGG WHITES

STRAWBERRY JELLY

Strawberry was one of the first jelly recipes we conquered. Back when we had real jobs we'd hit the wholesale market early to pick up crates of fruit. We would dress and juice the strawberries before heading into work – that way the fruit was in peak condition. We find that people really love real strawberry jelly. They are so conditioned by artificial strawberry flavors that the real flavor is a wake-up call.

So far, we have dealt with making jelly using easily obtainable juice. Some fruits are harder to juice than an orange, so you'll need a different method. The best way of getting juice out of soft fruits like strawberries and raspberries is to heat them gently in a bowl set over simmering water until the juices flood out.

Start by juicing the strawberries. It is easiest to do this a day ahead if possible. Hull and chop the strawberries and place in a heatproof bowl. Then add the sugar and the lemon juice. The lemon juice is important because it cuts through the richness of the strawberry juice and balances the flavor. Cover the top of the bowl with plastic wrap — make sure that both the bowl and plastic wrap are heat-resistant. Place the bowl above a pan of simmering water, and give it a good shake from time to time so that the strawberries are heated evenly. It will take about 30 minutes for the juice to be released.

You'll be left with a bowl of vibrantly colored juice and a whole heap of strawberry pulp. To separate the juice from the strawberries, it is best to use a jelly bag (available at www.canningpantry.com). A jelly bag is a very fine fabric sieve which, over the course of many hours, will let the

FOR GENEROUS 2 CUPS. SERVES 4

1LB RIPE STRAWBERRIES

¼ CUP SUPERFINE SUGAR

JUICE OF ½ LEMON

ABOUT 1¼ CUPS WATER

5 LEAVES OF GELATIN

RECIPE CONTINUES ON NEXT PAGE>

juice drip out beautifully clear. If you don't have a jelly bag, line a sieve with an old – but clean – piece of cheesecloth and set over a bowl. The juice will be at it clearest only if you let gravity do the work. If you're in a rush, you could use a few strokes of a wooden spoon to encourage the juice through – but don't go over the top.

Depending on the fruitiness of the strawberries, you should be left with a generous ¾ cup of juice. Add water to bring the volume up to 2 generous cups of liquid. (If you have less than that amount of juice, add more water.)

To set the jelly, cut up the gelatin and cover with about 2 tablespoons of the strawberry juice mixture and allow to soften. Then place over a pan of simmering water until it has dissolved. Finally add the rest of the strawberry juice mixture, stir, and then pass through a sieve into a suitable mold. Refrigerate until set.

A great use for the leftover strawberries (or indeed any other soft fruit) is to make them into a sorbet. It's really easy. Place the pulp in a food processor and combine with confectioners' sugar and the juice of a whole lemon until the mixture is smooth and sweet. Then tip into a shallow plastic container. Place this in the freezer and whisk vigorously with a fork every few hours until it is totally frozen. Easier still is to freeze it in an ice-cream machine.

RHUBARB AND ROSÉ JELLY

For this jelly recipe, you release the juice from the rhubarb by stewing it. Stewing also works well to release juice from fruits such as plums, cherries and blueberries. Many will be familiar with stewing rhubarb, but putting the juice to use in a jelly makes for a sublime experience. Even if it is pink and throbbing.

FOR GENEROUS 2 CUPS. SERVES 4

2LB 4OZ RHUBARB

GENEROUS ¾ CUP WATER

SCANT 1 CUP SUPERFINE SUGAR

1 STAR ANISE

JUICE OF ½ LEMON

½ CUP ROSÉ WINE OR WATER

5 LEAVES OF GELATIN

Wash and trim the rhubarb. Cut into 2-inch pieces, and add to a saucepan. Add the water, sugar and star anise. Bring to a boil and cover. Simmer until the rhubarb is really soft. This takes about 30 minutes.

Line a sieve with a piece of cheesecloth and set over a bowl. Transfer the rhubarb to the sieve and let the juice work its way through. You'll be left with a beautiful neon pink juice. To this, add the lemon juice.

Measure the volume of the rhubarb juice. If you are going down the rosé route, go for a generous 1½ cups of juice with ½ cup of rosé. Cheers! And if you are going the non-alcoholic route, use as much rhubarb juice as you have and add water as necessary until you reach a generous 2 cups.

Cut the leaves of gelatin into a few pieces and place in a heatproof bowl. Add a few tablespoons of the rhubarb mixture so the gelatin is just covered. Let the gelatin soften for 10 minutes while you bring a small pan of water to a simmer. Then place the bowl of softened gelatin over the simmering water and stir from time to time until totally melted.

Pour the remainder of the rhubarb mixture over the melted gelatin and stir to combine. Finally, pour the mixture through a sieve into a large measuring cup and then carefully fill your mold. Refrigerate until set.

CHERRY JELLY

Cherry jelly is really good. Sam thinks it's the best fruit jelly ever. This recipe uses a very fine cherry purée to create an unusual fruity texture. It's simple to make, because you can add the cherries directly to a saucepan without worrying about the pits.

Place the washed cherries into a saucepan and add the water and sugar. Bring to a boil, then cover and simmer gently until very soft – about 45 minutes.

Pass the juice through a sieve into a large measuring cup, pushing down with the back of a wooden spoon, until you have a bowl of rich cherry pulp. To this, add the lemon juice. Old recipes suggest that this is the time to add a brandy glass of Kirsch. This is suitably ambiguous, so interpret as you see fit. In any case, add additional water until you reach a generous 2 cups.

Cut the leaves of gelatin into a few pieces and place in a heatproof bowl. Add a few tablespoons of the cherry mixture so the gelatin is just covered. Let the gelatin soften for 10 minutes while you bring a small pan of water to a simmer. Then place the bowl of softened gelatin over the simmering water and stir from time to time until totally melted. Pour the remainder of the cherry mixture over the melted gelatin and stir.

Finally, pour the mixture through a sieve into a large measuring cup and then carefully fill your mold. Refrigerate until set.

FOR GENEROUS 2 CUPS, SERVES 4

SCANT 1LB CHERRIES

⅔ CUP WATER

HEAPING ⅓ CUP SUPERFINE SUGAR

JUICE OF ½ LEMON

ADDITIONAL WATER AND OPTIONAL KIRSCH

5 LEAVES OF GELATIN

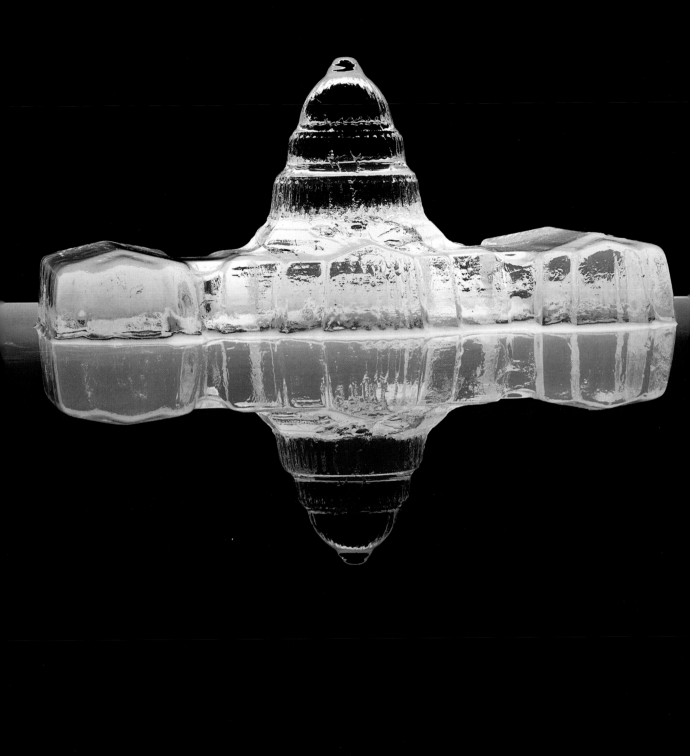

Greengage plum Jelly

It's a shame that greengages are in season for such a small part of the year becauses they are really tasty. In late summer, greengages make an unusual jelly. It's worth making extra and freezing the juice for later in the year.

Slice the greengages into quarters, removing the pits as you go, and place in a saucepan. Cover with the water and sugar, then bring to a boil and simmer, covered, until they have broken down — about 10 minutes.

Pour the contents into a sieve lined with cheesecloth placed over a large measuring cup. Use a wooden spoon to encourage the juices to go through, although this should happen without much difficulty. Once you have about 1¼ cups of juice, add the Riesling or water until you reach a generous 2 cups.

Cut the leaves of gelatin into a few pieces and place in a heatproof bowl. Add a few tablespoons of the juice mixture so the gelatin is just covered. Let the gelatin soften for 10 minutes while you bring a small pan of water to a simmer. Then place the bowl of softened gelatin over the simmering water and stir from time to time until totally melted. Pour the remainder of the greengage juice-mixture over the melted gelatin and stir to combine.

Finally, pour through a sieve into a large measuring cup and then carefully fill your mold. Place in the refrigerator to set.

For generous 2 cups, serves 4

1lb 2oz ripe greengages (or other plums)

generous ¾ cup water

¼ cup superfine sugar

¾ cup Riesling or water

5 leaves of gelatin

PINEAPPLE JELLY

Those used to getting adventurous making jelly for children may be familiar with the warning not to set fresh pineapple, papaya or kiwi fruit in the jelly . These exotic fruits all contain enzymes that attack gelatin and prevent it from forming a proper gel. In fact, bromelian, the enzyme in pineapple responsible for this, is literally flesh-eating! Fran Beauman, who has written at length on the subject, even reports that a particularly vicious pineapple can make your mouth bleed!

Flesh-eating aside, the history of the pineapple is quite intriguing. At one time, pineapples were so rare and in vogue that in 1761 a giant stone structure was built in the shape of one at Dunmore Park, Scotland. Back in the kitchen, it occurs again and again as a motif for jelly molds.

To make a pineapple jelly set, you need to denature the enzyme. Sounds complicated, but it only involves heating up the juice. This is why you can use canned pineapple in jelly – the fruit is pasteurized during canning.

FOR GENEROUS 2 CUPS, SERVES 4

1 LARGE RIPE PINEAPPLE

GENEROUS ¾ CUP WATER

HEAPING ⅓ CUP SUPERFINE SUGAR

JUICE OF 1 LIME

ADDITIONAL WATER (SEE RECIPE)

5 LEAVES OF GELATIN

Peel the pineapple and do your best to remove the eyes. Remove the core and discard. Cut the flesh into chunks and add to a saucepan. Then cover with the water and sugar and bring to a boil. Simmer gently, covered, until the pineapple is cooked right through – about 45 minutes.

Tip the stewed pineapple and juice into a sieve set over a large measuring cup. Add the lime juice and enough water until you reach a generous 2 cups.

Cut the gelatin into a few pieces and place in a heatproof bowl. Add a few tablespoons of the pineapple mixture so the gelatin is just covered. Let the gelatin soften for 10 minutes while you bring a small pan of water to a simmer. Place the bowl of softened gelatin over the simmering water and stir from time to time until totally melted. Then pour the remainder of the pineapple mixture over the melted gelatin and stir to combine.

Pour through a sieve into a large measuring cup and then carefully fill your mold. Refrigerate until set. If you wish you can set the stewed pineapple into the jelly (see method on p.64).

Tropical Jelly

For our tropical jelly, we've gone with pineapple, passion fruit, lemon, lime, and oranges – but there are infinitely more combinations up for grabs.

FOR GENEROUS 2 CUPS, SERVES 4

1 SMALL RIPE PINEAPPLE

JUICE OF 1 LARGE ORANGE

JUICE OF 1 LEMON

JUICE AND ZEST OF 1 LIME

3 PASSION FRUITS

WATER (SEE RECIPE)

5 LEAVES OF GELATIN

HEAPING ⅓ CUP SUPERFINE SUGAR

Start by dealing with the pineapple as in the recipe for Pineapple Jelly (see p.50).

Once you have the clear pineapple juice, pour it into a large measuring cup. Add the orange, lemon and lime juices, the lime zest, and then the juice of the passion fruits. Hold back the passion fruit seeds and set aside for later. If necessary, add water until you reach a generous 2 cups.

Cut the leaves of gelatin into a few pieces and place in a heatproof bowl. Add a few tablespoons of the juice mixture so the gelatin is just covered. Let the gelatin soften for 10 minutes while you bring a small pan of water to a simmer. Place the bowl of softened gelatin over the simmering water and stir from time to time until totally melted. Then pour the remainder of the juice mixture over the melted gelatin and stir to combine. Pour through a sieve into a bowl.

Set the bowl over a larger bowl filled with ice water. This will speed up the gelling process and allow the passion fruit seeds to be incorporated. After about 15 minutes, the mixture should be sufficiently gelled so that you can stir in the seeds without them sinking to the bottom. At this point, tip the jelly into a mold and place in the refrigerator to fully set.

Technique jellies

RIBBAND JELLY

Ribband Jelly is the traditional name for a striped jelly. In the past, making complex jellies often involved just one batch of jelly, which was divided so that flavors and colors could be added to create different jellies.

You can set any color of jelly in layers, although you will get the best results when you use a clear jelly in combination with an opaque jelly. That way, the colors don't merge into one. A raspberry and blancmange duo is a good place to start. Start by making the raspberry jelly and, while you are waiting for the juice to strain, get started on the blancmange jelly (recipes on page 59).

Choose a suitable mold and place it in the freezer to get it really cold. Something with a hole in the middle that can be filled with fruit and cream is fun. *This recipe will give you a 4 cup Ribband Jelly (which serves 8).*

TO ASSEMBLE THE RIBBAND JELLY

You should have two large measuring cups or pitchers of unset jelly and a thoroughly frozen mold.

Start by pouring a layer of the blancmange into the mold. Place in the refrigerator until set. This should take only 15 minutes.

Continue adding and setting contrasting layers to the jelly until it is full. You can make the layers as thin or thick as you like. Thin layers set more quickly but you will need to pour more of them; thicker layers set more slowly but there are fewer of them to do.

When all the layers are complete, continue to let the jelly chill for about another 2 hours to firm it up before unmolding and serving. A mound of whipped cream topped with a pile of raspberries will show off your spectacular creation best.

CONTINUES ON PAGE 59 >

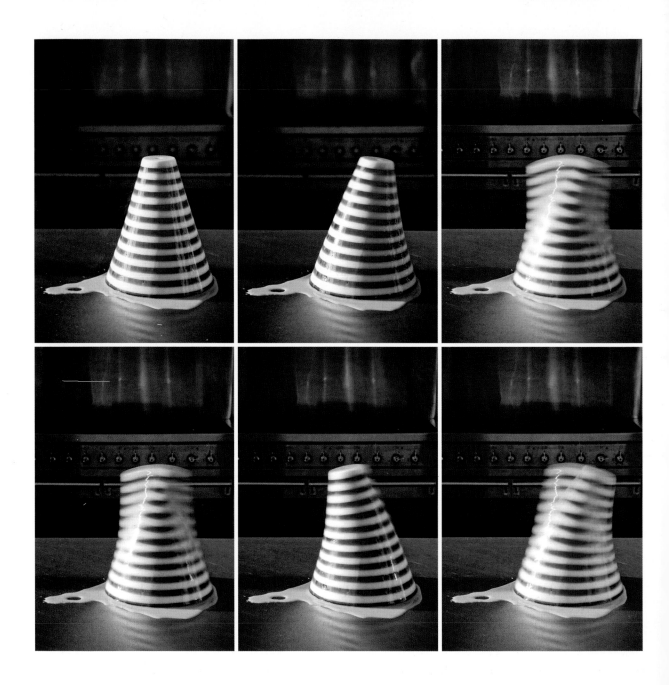

RASPBERRY JELLY

Rinse the raspberries and place them, along with the sugar, in a heatproof bowl. Cover tightly with plastic wrap and place on top of a pan of simmering water. Let the heat release the juices from the berries; this will take about 30 minutes. When you've got a nice pool of juice, pour everything into a sieve lined with a piece of cheesecloth over a large measuring cup and let the juice drip through clear.

Once the juice is strained, add the lemon juice and enough water until you reach a generous 2 cups.

Cut the gelatin into a few pieces and place in a heatproof bowl. Add a few tablespoons of the raspberry mixture so the gelatin is just covered. Let the gelatin soften for 10 minutes while you bring a small pan of water to a simmer. Place the bowl of gelatin over the simmering water and stir until totally melted. Pour the remainder of the raspberry mixture over the gelatin, stir to combine, and pass through a sieve into a large measuring cup or pitcher.

FOR GENEROUS 2 CUPS OF JELLY

1LB RIPE RASPBERRIES

HEAPING ⅓ CUP SUPERFINE SUGAR

JUICE OF ½ LEMON

ABOUT 1¼ CUPS WATER

5 LEAVES OF GELATIN

BLANCMANGE JELLY

Gelatin-based blancmanges made with whole milk will set a little firmer than fruit jelly, so it's OK to use a little less gelatin. This keeps the mouthfeel suitably soft.

Start by chopping the gelatin into a heatproof bowl and add 2 tablespoons of the water, along with the sugar and the lemon zest. Wait 10 minutes for the gelatin to soften and then heat over a pan of simmering water until the gelatin has melted. It is possible to melt the gelatin in the milk but it takes a long time – so it's easier to use water.

Once the gelatin has melted, add the rest of the water and milk to the bowl, stir to combine and pass everything through a sieve into a large measuring cup or pitcher.

FOR GENEROUS 2 CUPS OF BLANCMANGE

4 LEAVES OF GELATIN

SCANT ½ CUP WATER

1 TBSP SUPERFINE SUGAR

ZEST OF ½ LEMON

1¾ CUPS WHOLE MILK

MARBLED JELLY

Harry's always had an unhealthy fascination with the theory of taste embodied in marbled foods. Just think of Kobe beef or Stilton cheese: they look marbled and are full of flavor. The Victorians evidently thought so too, because they made marbled jellies. We found an old recipe for Marble Sweet Jelly while looking through *The Encyclopedia of Practical Cookery*, published in 1892. For a taste of how jelly recipes used to be written, here's the recipe quoted in full:

> MARBLED SWEET JELLY. *Get a jelly mould, put some pieces of different kinds of jelly at the bottom, over these pour some jelly that has had milk or cream mixed with it to make it white, so as to form the veins of the marble; the jelly should only just be liquid, for if it is too warm it will melt the other jelly, and spoil the effect. Let the jelly get cool as quickly as possible, then proceed as before, continuing in that way til the mould is full; pack the mould in ice and leave till the jelly is quite set. When ready, dip the mould in tepid water, wipe it, and turn the jelly out onto a glass dish.*

To make the marbled jelly, you need to make three different types of jelly. Two should be brightly colored and fully set before you start work on the blancmange part. It's a good way of using up any leftover jelly.

CONTINUES ON PAGE 62 >

MARBLED JELLY

Blueberry jelly and lemon jelly make a good combination to serve with this delicious cardamom and honey blancmange. Make these jellies first and ensure they are fully set before starting the blancmange. Use a half quantity of the recipe for Easy Lemon Jelly on p.36 to give you about 1 cup. *This recipe will give you a 4-cup Marbled Jelly (which serves 8).*

TO ASSEMBLE THE MARBLED JELLY

Gather your lemon and blueberry jellies. Turn them out onto a cutting board and cut them into small squares, triangles and strips. You need 1 cup of each chopped jelly.

Stir the blancmange mixture occasionally until it starts to get lumpy. This shouldn't take more than 15 minutes. At this point, you can add the chopped jelly and the almonds. The mixture is quite thick, so they will end up distributed evenly.

Pour the setting mixture into an elegant mold and place in the refrigerator. It will be ready to unmold in about 4 hours.

BLUEBERRY JELLY

Place the washed blueberries, water and sugar in a saucepan. Pop on a lid and stew for 10 minutes, or until the blueberries have split and lost their shape. Strain everything through a sieve and into a measuring cup until you have 1 cup of liquid (add water if necessary).

Cut up the gelatin into a heatproof bowl, add a little of the blueberry mixture and leave to soften. Place the softened bowl of gelatin over a pan of boiling water and allow to melt. Once melted, pour over the rest of the blueberry mixture and pour through a sieve back into the measuring cup.

If you want it to set quickly, pour thin layers onto a couple of dinner plates and refrigerate until firm.

FOR 1 CUP OF JELLY

HEAPING ¾ CUP BLUEBERRIES

SCANT ½ CUP WATER

2 TBSP SUPERFINE SUGAR

2½ LEAVES OF GELATIN

CARDAMOM & HONEY BLANCMANGE

First you need to infuse the milk. Put the milk in the saucepan with the cardamom, lemon zest and honey and heat until it is just about to simmer. Remove from the heat and allow the flavor to infuse as the mixture cools – about 20 minutes.

Meanwhile, cut the gelatin into a heatproof bowl and cover with the water. When the gelatin has softened, heat the mixture over simmering water until the gelatin is melted. Pour the infused milk over the melted gelatin and stir to combine, then pour through a sieve into a bowl.

Place the bowl over a larger bowl filled with ice.

FOR 2 CUPS OF BLANCMANGE

1¾ CUPS WHOLE MILK

10 CARDAMOM PODS

ZEST OF 1 LEMON

2 TBSP HONEY

4½ LEAVES OF GELATIN

½ CUP WATER

1 TBSP SLICED BLANCHED ALMONDS

SETTING FRUIT IN JELLY

Sometimes jelly is at its most stunning when it has fruit set inside it. We've found that one of the most popular recipes is elderflower jelly with raspberries set in it. If you can get hold of a combination of yellow and red raspberries, so much the better.

To make the elderflower jelly, you need to make up some elderflower cordial. Don't forget that flavors diminish with cold, so you need to make the cordial stronger than you would normally, otherwise, the taste might be too subtle. The joy of using cordial is that it is already a sugar syrup, so you won't need to add anything to make it sweeter.

ELDERFLOWER & RASPBERRY JELLY

FOR GENEROUS 2 CUPS

⅔ CUP ELDERFLOWER CORDIAL

1½ CUPS WATER

5 LEAVES OF GELATIN

¾ CUP RASPBERRIES
OR OTHER SOFT FRUIT

First, in a large measuring cup, mix the cordial with the water. Cut up the gelatin and add to a heatproof bowl. Cover with a splash of the cordial and leave for 10 minutes to soften. Then place the bowl over a pan of simmering water and allow the gelatin to melt. Next, pour over the remainder of the cordial, stir and pass through a sieve back into the measuring cup.

Carefully rinse the raspberries to remove any dirt and discard any overly soft berries, then place them into the mold.

When you have made up the jelly, you can begin filling the mold. Carefully half-fill the mold. Raspberries are fairly buoyant, so if you half-fill the mold and then allow this to set, you will end up with a jelly with fruit held aloft.

Meanwhile, keep the remaining mixture at room temperature. After a couple of hours in the refrigerator, the jelly will have set sufficiently for you to pour the remainder of the mixture into the mold. (On a really cold day, the cordial in the measuring cup might start to gel. If this happens, melt it by putting the measuring cup in a pan of hot water for a few minutes.) Once the final layer has set, you are ready to unmold.

Mosaic jelly

A mosaic made of jelly is one of the most spectacular things you can do without a complex mold. The idea is that you line the interior of the mold with thin tiles of jelly. Of course, the mosaic can be as complicated as you like. A good way to start is to use cookie cutters to create the jelly tiles. We've used a fleur-de-lis cutter, which we designed. Harry got it made on a machine that is normally used for making replacement body parts, titanium hip joints and the like. You can use anything you want. Alter the colors and shapes to suit the occasion. Or cut out shapes with a knife.

Sticking cut-out shapes onto the interior of a mold is quite an art, so to get started it's easier to make the jelly on a flat tray. The results are still spectacular. Once you are good at it, try molds with curved or domed sides.

FOR THE JELLY TILES

Start by making a blancmange jelly (p.59) and setting the jelly into thin (slightly thinner than ¼ inch) sheets on a flat, and super clean, baking pan. It may be easier to use a series of flat dinner plates. Make the jelly using 5 leaves of gelatin per 2 generous cups of liquid so that it is a bit firmer. This will make it easier to cut and lift the shapes.

Choose a flat dish in which to set the jelly. Metal baking pans really do work best here because it is easier to stick the jelly shapes onto them.

ASSEMBLING THE MOSAIC

Carefully cut out shapes from the blancmange and transfer them to the dish using a metal spatula. Then arrange the shapes as you see fit. Place back in the refrigerator for 30 minutes to firm up a little.

Carefully fill the dish with a jelly of your choice. If you are using white tiles, a strawberry jelly would make a good contrast. The trick is to get the filling jelly a little syrupy before adding it, which stops the mosaic from floating away.

Once set, serve at the table to amaze your dinner guests.

Striped clementine jellies

Many people will remember eating sailboats made from jelly set inside oranges, with sails made from rice paper and toothpicks. In fact, setting jelly into hollowed-out oranges has quite a heritage. The great chef Antonin Carême made the ultimate combination, magically setting thin layers of jelly inside hollowed-out clementines. We picked up this technique from the wonderful food historian Ivan Day. Try it! It's not as complicated as it looks and the results are spectacular. Make sure that you reveal the layered jelly with a ceremonial slicing at the table.

When you are out shopping, choose clementines that have lots of give in the peel. Otherwise, this recipe is just no fun.

1. HOLLOWING OUT THE CLEMENTINES

First find the right end of the clementine: you want the part that sticks out a little and has the dark, hard bit where it was attached to the tree. Use a small knife to remove a circle of peel slightly bigger than ¼ inch in diameter. From this, you are going to hollow out the clementine.

Using a small teaspoon, carefully remove the segments from the clementines. Once you've got the first segment out, it gets easier. Keep removing the flesh until the clementine is cleanly hollowed out. Don't worry if you create small holes; these can be fixed. But don't rip the sides, so careful as you go! Place the flesh into a bowl. This will be made into the clementine jelly. Meanwhile, refrigerate the clementine skins. This will make setting the layers quicker.

2. MAKING THE CLEMENTINE JELLY

Pass the clementine flesh through the sieve and into a measuring cup until you have obtained all the juices. Now add half sugar syrup and half water until you have doubled the liquid in volume. Use the Universal

CONTINUES ON PAGE 70 >

10 CLEMENTINES

SUGAR SYRUP (P.29), QUANTITY TO SUIT (SEE
METHOD)

WATER, QUANTITY TO SUIT (SEE METHOD)

GELATIN LEAVES, QUANTITY TO SUIT (SEE UNIVERSAL
PRINCIPLE, P.24—28)

FOR THE BLANCMANGE:

8 LEAVES OF GELATIN

¾ CUP WATER

1 TBSP SUPERFINE SUGAR

ZEST OF ½ LEMON

SCANT 3½ CUPS MILK

Jelly Principle (see p.24–28) to add the correct quantity of gelatin and get the jelly mixture made up. Keep this in a large measuring cup or a jug.

3. MAKING THE BLANCMANGE

Make up an equal quantity of blancmange, following the recipe on p.59.

4. FIXING ANY HOLES IN THE CLEMENTINES

The next stage is to fix any tiny holes in the bottom of the clementines. We're going to block them with jelly. To do this, take a few tablespoons of the clementine jelly, then put it into a glass and place in the refrigerator. Don't forget about it. In about 15 minutes, it will have gelled enough so that it can be used to block the holes. You want it lumpy but still just about flowing. Place a small amount of the clementine jelly into any holes that need blocking and place back in the refrigerator until fully set. This will take about 15 minutes.

5. SETTING THE LAYERS

Once you are watertight, you can get going on the layers. For the first layer, measure 2 teaspoons of clementine jelly and pour it into the clementines. Allow to set. The layers are thin, so this should take no more than 30 minutes. Then follow with 1 tablespoon of the blancmange and again allow to set.

If any of the jelly in the measuring cups begins to gel during this process, heat it up gently by immersing the cup in a pan of lukewarm water.

Keep adding alternate layers of jelly until the clementines are full. Try to end with a clementine layer.

6. THE REVEAL

To serve, simply slice the clementines top to bottom into quarters to reveal the magical stripes. Eat like orange quarters.

It is, of course, possible to do this with other flavors, but it does make sense to use the juice that you get from the clementines. Mixing the orange juice with some strawberry juice works well, because it increases the color contrast with the blancmange.

GOLD LEAF IN JELLIES

Cooking with gold leaf is a total extravagance. It doesn't improve the jelly because it has no smell or perceptible taste, and it is a complete bore to handle. It does, however, massively increase the impact of the jelly. The extravagance of eating 24-karat gold adds excitement, and it looks splendid if done properly.

If you have any qualms about eating gold, don't worry. It's totally inert and the United States recognizes it as a food additive, though this rather knocks the glamor out of it. More surprising, as it's inert your body can't digest it – and you can imagine what that means.

Gold leaf has a glorious history in cooking. In the Middle Ages, whole birds, pâtés, and pigs' heads were wrapped in gold leaf for feasting. In 1769, Elizabeth Raffald wrote a recipe for gilded fish in jelly. Once you've unmolded your fish you carefully lay gold leaf onto them, arrange them in a dish and flood the plate with jelly. These days, gold is used sparingly to decorate chocolates and liqueurs. But once you finish reading this segment, you will be able to achieve far more spectacular effects with gold.

You can get hold of gold from large art supply stores or even on Amazon.com. It comes in three different formats: gold leaf, gold ribbon,and gold dust. We use gold leaf because it is the best value for money at under $2.00 per leaf. You get 25 leaves per booklet and it represents the best return on investment in terms of absolute impact.

The higher karat of gold, the better. Anything above 22-karat gold is edible, but the closer it is to 24-karat, the better. Below 24 karats, the gold is mixed with copper and nickel. We tend to use 22.5-karat gold.

See pages 24–25 for the technique.

SETTING GOLD LEAF
IN A GEL

Rather than make a jelly recipe that has gold throughout, it is often most effective to concentrate the gold at the top of the jelly for maximum impact. If you are going to unmold your jelly, put the gold gel in first; if the jelly is being served inside a glass, put it in last.

ENOUGH TO TIP 10 SMALL JELLIES

2 LEAVES OF GELATIN

½ CUP PROSECCO OR SUGAR SYRUP

10 SHEETS OF GOLD LEAF

Sam likes to set gold gel firmer than the rest of the jelly; Harry thinks this is a habit gained from the first gold jellies that Sam made – they were jelly breasts with golden nipples. For best results, you want the gold leaf suspended throughout the gel, and for this to happen the gel has to thicken slightly. This is super-quick if you have a higher gel to fluid ratio.

Cut the gelatin into a heatproof bowl, add a splash of prosecco and let the leaves soften. Melt the gelatin over a pan of simmering water, add the rest of the prosecco and strain back into a bowl or large measuring cup.

Now you have the gel to which you can add the gold. Gold leaf is only a few atoms thick, so it's very fragile. You need to manipulate 10 leaves of it from its booklet and into the mixture. You could use a gilders tip (made out of squirrel hair), but we tend to use a fork with a slightly damp tine.

Hold the booklet of gold leaf right over the bowl. Use the moistened fork to pick up corners of gold leaf and pull them into the liquid. Gold leaf will stick to anything it lands on, so try to get it into the liquid the first time.

When the 10 sheets of gold leaf are in the bowl, use a whisk to beat it up. The aim is to break up the gold leaf into tiny fragments that will catch the light, but to avoid introducing air bubbles into the mix. Tilt the bowl to pick up any gold leaf that has stuck to the sides and beat it in.

When the gold leaf has been broken up to a size you are happy with, lower the temperature of the mixture by holding it over an ice bath or by placing it in your refrigerator; allow it to gel sufficiently so that when the gold is stirred around it no longer sinks to the bottom of the mixture. When it is at this consistency, pour it swiftly into the mold and refrigerate until set.

If the gelling goes too far and the mixture sets (or is too thick to pour), you can rescue it! Jelly is very forgiving. Hold the bowl in another bowl of hot water and stir until it reaches the desired consistency. *See the Funeral Jelly recipe on p.112 for a full recipe with gold.*

ALCOHOLIC JELLIES

WEDDING JELLY

Wedding cakes are all stodge and no fun. It's inexplicable that people spend so much on vast monstrosities of fruit cake shrouded in royal icing. After all, most of it never gets eaten. It's trodden into the dance floor, stuffed in purses, and left forgotton in an attic in anticipation of a christening. Wedding jellies, on the other hand, are lighter and more refreshing than fruit cakes. And they are kinder to the stomach after a heavy meal, making it less likely that guests will fall asleep duing the speeches!

After making a towering jelly for the wedding of Sam's cousin, we decided to launch a wedding jelly service. There's been a freeing up of what's acceptable to serve at weddings, and we've been to events where cheese, cupcakes and even savory meat pies are served in lieu of a wedding cake.

Try the following recipe for a Champagne and summer fruit wedding jelly and your guests won't be disappointed.

CHAMPAGNE & SUMMER FRUIT WEDDING JELLY

A bottle of Champagne will make enough jelly for four proper servings and a glass for yourself while you are cooking. Make sure to chill the Champagne ahead of time – it's important that you drink while on the job.

GENEROUS 2 CUPS, ENOUGH FOR 4

5 LEAVES OF GELATIN

SCANT 2 CUPS CHAMPAGNE OR
SPARKLING WINE

SCANT ¼ CUP SUPERFINE SUGAR

A SQUEEZE OF LEMON JUICE

A HANDFUL OF SMALL FRUIT
(BLUEBERRIES, RASPBERRIES, GRAPES
...WHATEVER LOOKS GOOD)

Cut the gelatin into a heatproof bowl with a pair of scissors. Add enough Champagne to cover (about a scant ½ cup). Leave the gelatin to soften for 10 minutes.

Bring a pan of water to a boil and place the bowl of softened gelatin on top of the pan of boiling water. Once the gelatin has totally melted, stir in the sugar until it has dissolved and add another scant ½ cup of Champagne to the mixture.

Pour the mixture through a sieve – to remove any unmelted lumps – into a large measuring cup. Squeeze the lemon through the sieve too. Add enough of the remaining Champagne until you have reached a generous 2 cups.

Place the washed fruit into the bottom of the mold and pour in about one-third of the jelly. Put the mold in the refrigerator for the jelly to set. Leave until set enough so that the fruit seems safely embedded (about 2 hours), then pour over the rest of the jelly mixture and return to the refrigerator.

If you don't want to set the fruit in the mold first, you can always add everything to the mold at once. Doing a double set, however, makes sure that the fruit floats elegantly in the unmolded jelly rather than sinking to the bottom. For a way of keeping all the fizz in the Champagne, see p.132.

ABSINTHE JELLY RONSON

We created Jelly Ronson for musician Mark Ronson's 33rd birthday party. Historically, chefs have named foods to honor patrons. Antonin Carême created a Soufflé Rothschild in the 1820s and Auguste Escoffier, chef of the Savoy Hotel, created Peach Melba in the early 1890s to honor the Australian soprano Dame Nellie Melba. It's still popular.

This alcoholic jelly is fully potent. Sam likes to serve it to make sure that parties kick-off right; things can get a little wild after it's introduced. If you are making it for a party, it's worthwhile covering any paintings and wall decorations you value. If this jelly is served after 11p.m., food *will* be thrown. Remember, 11p.m. is the witching hour for throwing food.

Prepare this at least a day before serving, which leaves you free on the day to organize your party.

For the Jelly

⅔ CUP ABSINTHE (BOHEMIAN ABSINTHE PREFERRED)

1¼ CUPS TONIC WATER

JUICE OF ½ LIME

SCANT ¼ CUP SUGAR SYRUP

5 LEAVES OF GELATIN

For the Raspberry Coulis

HEAPING ⅓ CUP RASPBERRIES

JUICE OF ½ LEMON

1 TSP CONFECTIONERS' SUGAR

Combine the absinthe, tonic water, lime juice and sugar syrup in a large measuring cup and set aside. Cut the leaf gelatin into pieces and place in a heatproof bowl with enough of the absinthe cocktail to submerse. Leave until soft.

When the gelatin has softened, melt it by placing the bowl over a pan of simmering water. Then add the remainder of the absinthe cocktail from the measuring cup, give it a brief stir, and pour everything through a sieve and back into the measuring cup. Find a suitably extravagent mold and fill it with the mixture. Refrigerate overnight to set – now you've got a whole day to cover up those paintings.

We serve this with a raspberry coulis.

Place the raspberries, lemon juice, and confectioners' sugar into a mini-food processor and whizz until smooth. Use a spoon to force the coulis through a sieve, into a bowl and then into a small pitcher for pouring. Job done!

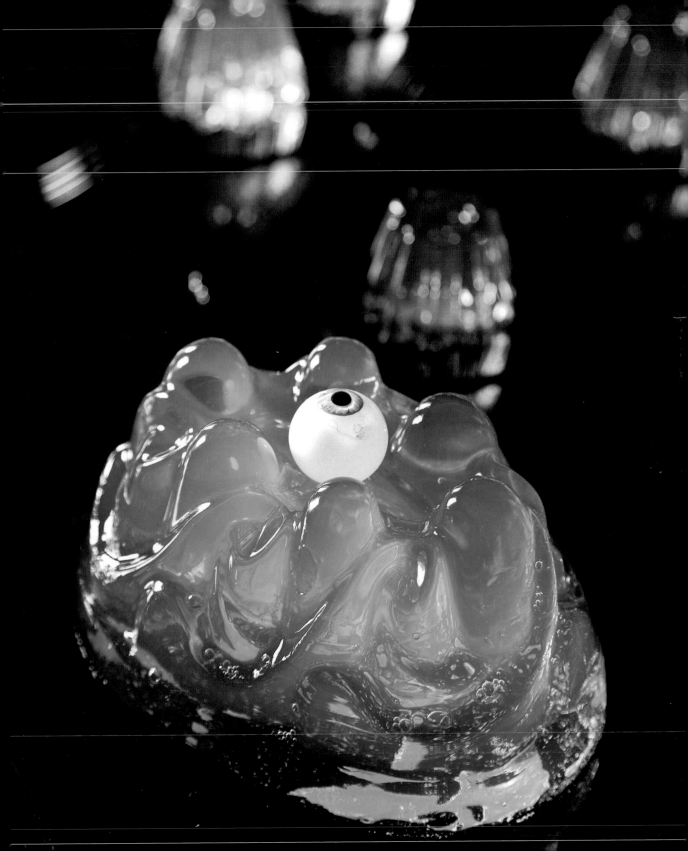

TITANIC JELLY

For 2,000 years, last suppers have been some of the most interesting meals around. Everyone has a last supper waiting for them, though most don't feature jelly. Some death row inmates have had a crack but their jellies have been pretty unambitious; the same is not true of the jellies that were eaten by passengers the night the *Titanic* sank. The story of the *Titanic* is endlessly fascinating; after all, this is still the ultimate shipwreck. Only two menus survive from the night of April 14, 1912. The menu from First Class features a jelly for the tenth course. One of the passengers, Mrs. Jacques Futrelle, described the scene:

> *There was not the slightest thought of danger in the minds of those who sat around the tables in the luxurious dining saloon of the* Titanic. *It was a brilliant crowd. Jewels flashed from the gowns of the women. And, oh, the dear women, how fondly they wore their latest Parisian gowns! It was the first time that most of them had an opportunity to display their newly acquired finery.*

The guests that tasted the jelly that night included some of the ship's most renowned passengers: John Jacob Astor, Benjamin Guggenheim, and Isidor and Ida Straus. It was a splendid feast, and by the time they got to the jelly they would have been stuffed. No doubt they would have been grateful to be presented with a light peach and chartreuse jelly before getting stuck into coffee and cigars. If you are having a last supper, you could do a lot worse.

Several hours later, in the early morning of April 15, the *Titanic* sank, taking 1,581 passengers and crew with her. The band played the hymn "Nearer, My God, To Thee" as the ship went down.

CONTINUES ON PAGE 88 >

CHARTREUSE & PEACH JELLY

This recipe is taken from the surreal book *Last Dinner on the Titanic*. Every year groups of enthusiasts recreate the menus from the doomed liner and even get involved in aristocratic role-play. This jelly is good with cigars and impending doom at the end of the meal.

For Poached Peaches

2 LARGE PEACHES

GENEROUS 2 CUPS WATER

1¼ CUPS SUPERFINE SUGAR

2 WHOLE CLOVES

1 CINNAMON STICK

JUICE OF ½ LEMON

For the Jelly

FOR GENEROUS 2 CUPS.
ENOUGH FOR 4

GENEROUS ¾ CUP
CHARTREUSE LIQUEUR

1 CUP WATER

SCANT ¼ CUP PEACH POACHING
SYRUP/SUGAR SYRUP

5 LEAVES OF GELATIN

PEACHES AS PREPARED ABOVE. OR
SCANT ½ CUP CANNED PEACHES

FOR THE POACHED PEACHES

First, peel the peaches by immersing them in boiling water for 30 seconds. Take them out and plunge them into cold water before removing the skins, halving the fruit and taking out the pits. Combine the water and sugar in a pan and heat until the sugar has dissolved. Add the cloves, cinnamon and lemon juice. Bring the syrup just to a boil and then reduce the heat. Add the peaches and poach for 6 minutes, or until they are soft. Remove the peaches, but don't throw away the syrup.

FOR THE JELLY

In a large measuring cup, combine the liqueur, water, and a scant ¼cup of the poaching syrup.

Cut the gelatin into a heatproof bowl and add enough water to cover. Leave the gelatin to soften for 10 minutes.

Bring a pan of water to a boil and place the bowl of softened gelatin on top of the pan. Once the gelatin has totally melted, add the Chartreuse mixture and give it a quick stir.

Pour a shallow layer of the mixture into the mold and leave in the refrigerator for 1–2 hours, or until it is set. Pour a very thin layer of jelly on top and arrange a fan of sliced peaches on the jelly. Return to the refrigerator briefly until the peaches are held in place. Add another layer of jelly (thicker this time) and set another layer of peaches in place. Repeat until you've used all the mixture.

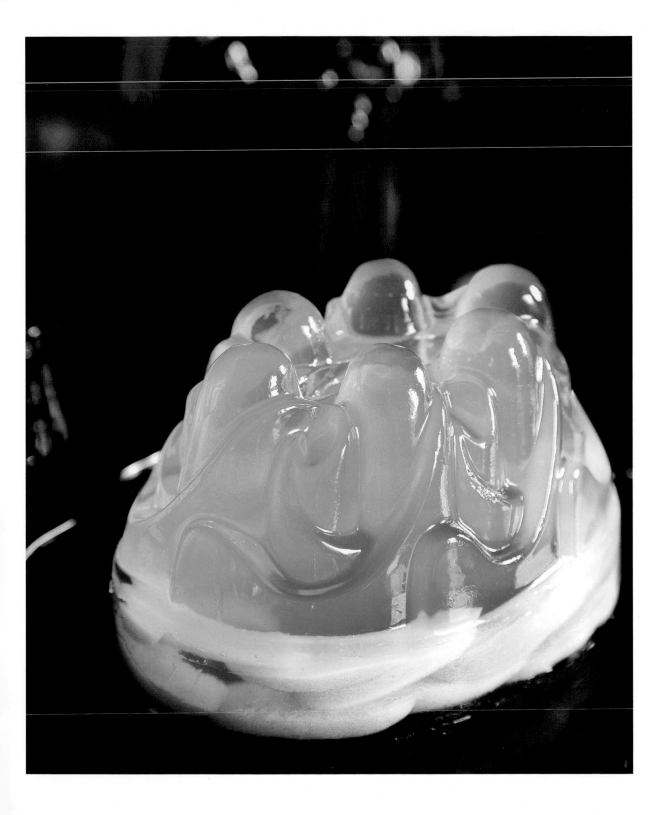

ALCOHOL INFUSIONS

Everyone loves candy. When Saddam Hussein was captured in 2003, he was found with $750,000, a chicken and two Bounty Bars stashed in his refrigerator. We have a lot of fun turning popular candy into smashing jellies using an alcohol solvent to extract the flavor.

Alcohol is an excellent solvent for volatile aromatic molecules. It does a good job of extracting and holding onto flavor from solid ingredients, ranging from herbs and fruits to nuts, spices and flowers. Leave anything in alcohol long enough, and it will extract the flavor. You can even do Snickers® or Mars® Bars.

When you are starting out, it makes sense to use vodka as the solvent. It has little flavor of its own, so your extracts will be purer. Because you are filling the vodka chockfull of the flavors and colors of your choice, buy the cheapest vodka available. You may get marginally better results from premium spirits, but you'll pay a vastly increased price to do so.

BUBBLEGUM VODKA JELLY

In the United States, "molecular mixologist" Eban Freeman makes a bubble gum cocktail by infusing vodka with Bazooka Joe® Bubble Gum. It's pretty saccharine sweet. In the U.K., Anglo Bubbly is used to infuse vodka to make a lurid pink, bubblegum jelly. (Please note: The egg whites in this recipe are not cooked. If salmonella is a problem in your area, use a liquid egg white product.)

FOR THE INFUSION

Unwrap the bubblegum and chop into small pieces the size of your little finger nail. Then submerge in the vodka and leave in a covered container for 48 hours, shaking occasionally. The original vodka bottle makes a handy container if nothing else is handy.

Strain the mixture through coffee-filter paper to remove the "crud." You will be left with an acid-pink vodka, flavored with bubblegum. This can be kept in a sealed container indefinitely.

FOR THE JELLY

Place the bubblegum vodka in a large measuring cup and add the lemon juice, lime juice, syrup and water. You can adjust the proportions to taste, but make sure that you end up with a generous 2 cups of liquid.

Cut the leaf gelatin into a heatproof bowl and add enough of this mixture to cover. Let the gelatin soften for 10 minutes.

Bring a pan of water to a boil and place the bowl of soft gelatin on top of the pan of boiling water. Once the gelatin has melted, add some of the remaining vodka mixture to the bowl. Give it a stir and then pour the entire contents through a sieve and into a bowl.

Set the bowl over a larger bowl filled with iced water and add the egg whites to the jelly. Using an electric beater, whisk the mixture until there is a layer of foam on top. Pour immediately into eight glasses and place in the refrigerator to set.

For the infusion
(to extract the flavor)

10 PIECES OF BUBBLEGUM

1 CUP VODKA

For the Bubblegum Jelly

FOR GENEROUS 2 CUPS, ENOUGH FOR 8

GENEROUS ¾ CUP INFUSED VODKA

JUICE OF ½ LEMON

JUICE OF ½ LIME

¼ CUP SUGAR SYRUP

¾ CUP WATER

4 LEAVES OF GELATIN

3 EGG WHITES

STRIPED SKITTLES JELLY

The bubblegum technique works wonders using Skittles® too. A good look is creating five infused vodkas, each one from different colored Skittles. You can make them up individually or layer them up all together to create Neopolitan-style rainbow slices as described below.

For the Skittles Infusions

4 PACKS OF SKITTLES

3⅓ CUPS VODKA

For the Jelly

FOR GENEROUS
2 CUPS, ENOUGH FOR 8

SKITTLES-INFUSED VODKA

JUICE OF 1 LIME

SCANT ¼ CUP WATER

SUGAR SYRUP, TO TASTE

10 LEAVES OF GELATIN

FOR THE INFUSIONS

Start by finding five small containers with tight-fitting lids that will each hold ⅔ cup of liquid. A tupperware set could do the trick. Open the packs of Skittles and separate out the colors into the five containers. Then pour over each one ⅔ cup of vodka. Seal the containers and leave for 48 hours, shaking occasionally.

Strain the flavored vodka through coffee filter paper into five large glasses.

FOR THE JELLY

Place scant ½ cup Skittle vodka in a measuring cup and add a squeeze of lime juice, the water and syrup to taste. If you like it sour, add more lime juice. If you like it sweet, add more syrup. Make sure you end up with a generous ¾ cup of liquid.

Cut 2 leaves of gelatin into a heatproof bowl and add enough of the Skittle vodka mixture to cover. Leave the gelatin to soften while you bring a pan of water to a boil. Place the bowl of softened gelatin on top of the pan of boiling water.

Once the gelatin has melted, add some of the vodka mixture to the bowl. Stir and then pour it all through a sieve back into the measuring cup.

You can effectively make all of the jellies at the same time if you have enough bowls. Just put them one at time over the boiling water. It's quicker than you might imagine.

Pour one of the jellies into a loaf pan and place in the refrigerator to set. Once set, continue adding layers in the same way. To serve, unmold the jelly and, using a knife dipped in hot water, carefully cut slices crossways.

LAVENDER JELLY

This jelly is a tart fella and uses a gin base to extract the lavender flavor. It's based on a recipe for the gin gimlet cocktail.

FOR THE INFUSION

Break up the lavender and submerge in the gin in a container. Cover and leave to stand for 48 hours, shaking occasionally. Strain the mixture through a fine wire sieve to remove the pieces.

FOR THE LAVENDER JELLY

Place the gin, lime juice, syrup and water in a large measuring cup or pitcher.

Cut the leaf gelatin into a heatproof bowl and add enough of this mixture to cover. Leave the gelatin to soften for 10 minutes. Bring a pan of water to a boil and once the gelatin has softened, place the heatproof bowl on top of the pan of boiling water.

Once the gelatin has melted, add the rest of the mixture to the bowl. Stir and then pour the entire contents through a sieve into the large measuring cup or pitcher.

Pour this mixture into a mold and place in the refrigerator to set.

For the infusion
(to extract the flavor)
¾OZ FRESH LAVENDER

1 CUP GIN

For the Lavender Jelly
(serves 8)
1 CUP LAVENDER-INFUSED GIN

½ CUP FRESHLY SQUEEZED LIME JUICE

SCANT ⅓ CUP SUGAR SYRUP

SCANT ¼ CUP WATER

5 LEAVES OF GELATIN

FUTURIST BANQUET

The Futurists were utterly wild and totally ahead of their time. They were banging on about multisensory dining experiences decades before it was fashionable. Their *Futurist Cookbook* written in 1932 contains not only "recipes" and manifestos but also some unreal descriptions of banquets. We particularly like the airplane banquet, where the main course of "pork fuselage" arrives to a symphony of real airplane engines firing up.

For the 100th anniversary of Futurism in 2009, we worked with The Olde Bell Inn, Berkshire, to create our own aero-banquet. Over the course of the meal guests had their coats transformed into cocktails, experienced a plane crash and were served jelly out of the back of an ambulance amid the blazing wreckage.

Campari & orange jelly bombe

For the Campari Jelly

THIS RECIPE MAKES A
GENEROUS 2 CUPS, BUT ADJUST THE
QUANTITIES AS NECESSARY

5 LEAVES OF GELATIN

SCANT ½ CUP CAMPARI

GENEROUS ¾ CUP SUGAR SYRUP

GENEROUS ¾ CUP CLUB SODA

PLUS 1 QUANTITY OF
ORANGE JELLY (P.34)

We developed this recipe when we were lucky enough to be asked to make the dessert for a Futurist Banquet held in New York. This recipe is our take on the Futurist Bombe. Bombes, usually ice-cream based, have a hidden inner core of a different flavor. We made a jelly bombe by creating a mold within a mold. The results are spectacular and easily replicable at home. The outer layer is a bright Campari red and the inner layer is an opaque orange jelly. It will astound your guests.

You will need two molds, one to fit inside the other. We made a special two-part mold for ourselves, but you can make an impromptu bombe mold with a set of Tupperware bowls. You need two bowls, one with a diameter about 1½ inches smaller than the other. Best to read through the technique below to get familiar with the process before embarking on making this one.

WORKING OUT VOLUMES

Use a measuring cup to work out the volumes of the large and the small molds. Then subtract one from the other to give you the volume of Campari Jelly required to fill the gap between the larger and smaller molds. Write down the volume of the smaller mold – and keep your note safe!

PREPARING THE TWO-PART MOLD

Place the large bowl on a small tray and then use a couple of rulers to suspend the smaller bowl over the larger. Now fill the small bowl with something heavy: coins, ceramic baking beans, rice, etc. This will stop it from floating away when you pour in the jelly.

CONTINUES ON PAGE 100 >

CAMPARI JELLY

Chop the gelatin into a heatproof bowl. Mix up the liquids and pour a little over the gelatin. When the gelatin has softened place the bowl over a pan of boiling water and allow the gelatin to melt.

Pour the rest of the campari mixture into the bowl, stir and pour through a sieve back into a pitcher or large measuring cup. To make it set a little quicker, you can stir the mixture over ice until it thickens.

Pour the jelly into the gap between the larger and smaller molds. Allow this to set completely – about 3 hours.

ORANGE JELLY

Use the recipe for Orange Jelly on p.34 to make up the correct volume of jelly. You can do this while the Campari Jelly is setting and leave it out of the refrigerator until required. If it starts to solidify, melt it by placing the pitcher in a pan of lukewarm water and stirring occasionally.

REMOVING THE INNER MOLD AND CASTING
THE ORANGE JELLY

Once the Campari Jelly has set, carefully tip out the content of the inner mold and fill it with warm water. Wait for about 20 seconds, then pull out the inner mold. It might help to twist it as you pull because there will be a fair bit of suction. You will be left with a hollow that can now be filled with the Orange Jelly. Fill it right up flush with the top of the Campari Jelly. Carefully place in the refrigerator until fully set.

UNMOLDING

Unmold the jelly by dipping the large bowl into warm water and inverting. Serve with slices of orange.

JELLY
COCKTAILS

Anything liquid can be made into a jelly. As such, cocktails provide a galaxy of inspiration. If you go into a bar and like what you are drinking, turn it into a jelly. Just make your concoction, add some gelatin, and refrigerate. The results can be spectacular.

The inspiration goes both ways. Bartenders are taking their inspiration from chefs and turning cocktails into jellies. It's big fad at the moment, though the bartenders have a habit of calling these jellies "solids." This is disgusting and should be stopped right away; the word has foul associations.

In this section, we'll show you how to turn a few simple cocktails into jellies. Once you have mastered these, you'll be able to turn any cocktail into a jelly.

MAI TAI

Jelly has a strong visual component, so let's start off by looking at how a Mai Tai can be turned into a jelly.

The Mai Tai is a rum-based cocktail associated with Tiki culture. It's a potent drink, so as a jelly it should be treated with respect. Having said that, the Tiki styling associated with the Mai Tai is enormously silly. The drink was initially served in outlandishly decorated bars stuffed full of imitation stone heads, bamboo DJ booths and alligators strapped to the ceiling. See page 105 for some ideas for attempting your own Tiki styling.

"Trader Vic" Bergeron claims the laurels for the drink's invention. There's been some dispute about who really came up with the concoction, but this apparently "makes his ulcer burn," so let's give Vic credit. Whatever the case, the cocktail was popularized through his global chain of high-kitsch concept bars. They still peddle them today.

Be warned: this jelly will get you bongoed.

Combine the rum, curacao, orgeat syrup, sugar syrup and lime juice in a pitcher as if you were about to make a Mai Tai cocktail.

Cut the leaf gelatin into a heatproof bowl and add enough of the Mai Tai mixture to cover. Leave the gelatin to soften for 10 minutes. Bring a pan of water to a boil and, once the gelatin has softened, place the heatproof bowl on top of the pan of boiling water.

Once the gelatin has totally melted, add some of the rest of the Mai Tai mixture to the bowl. Stir and then pour the whole lot through a sieve and into the pitcher.

Pour this mixture into a mold or glasses and set it in the refrigerator.

When you are ready to serve, unmold and garnish with the sprig of mint.

Mai Tai — based on the original Trader Vic Formula (1944)
SERVES 4

1 CUP MEDIUM JAMAICAN RUM

5 TBSP ORANGE CURACAO

5 TBSP ORGEAT SYRUP

SCANT ¼ CUP SUGAR SYRUP

SCANT ¼ CUP LIME JUICE

5 LEAVES OF GELATIN

SPRIG OF FRESH MINT, TO GARNISH

Making your
Living Room
Into a Tiki Den

Mai Tais are served in outlandishly decorated bars, so some of the flavor will come from the setting. A paper published in 2003 by Professor John Edwards found that the dish *chicken à la king* tasted different depending on the environment where it was eaten. The dish was tasted in schools, residential homes and swanky restaurants. The better the environment, the better the dish tasted. By extension, the more exotic the location you serve your Mai Tai jelly in, the more exotic it will taste. Just remember that history lesson we gave you earlier about banqueting houses – there was a reason for designing buildings just to house desserts.

SAM'S TIP FOR HOW TO TURN YOUR LIVING ROOM
INTO A TIKI DEN:

A good place to start is Cheeky Tiki (www.cheekytiki.com) for inspiration. Here you can also load up on Samoan war clubs, porcupine fish and hand-carved tikis. If your budget doesn't stretch to this, you'll have to go down to the garden center and buy a load of bamboo. Split it and stick it to every surface and all over the furniture in your front room. When you have done this, you can welcome your friends to your Tiki den. Watch their jaws drop!

PIMMS CUP

A good summer jelly for displaying your prowess at setting fruit. Alternatively, omit the fruit and make a delicious plain jelly, as we made for the picture.

Combine the Pimms, lemonade, and ginger ale in a pitcher as if you were about to make a pitcher of Pimms. Squeeze in the lemon juice.

Cut the fine-leaf gelatin into a heatproof bowl and add enough of the Pimm's mixture to cover. Leave the gelatin to bloom for 10 minutes. Bring a pan of water to a boil and place the bowl of softened gelatin on top.

Once the gelatin has totally melted, add the rest of the Pimm's mixture to the bowl. Stir, then pour through a sieve into the pitcher.

Pour a shallow layer of the mixture into your mold and add a layer of fruit and/or cucumber. Put the mold in the refrigerator for the jelly to set. Once set, repeat this until you've used up all the jelly and fruit and/or cucumber.

When you are ready to serve, unmold and garnish with the sprig of mint.

SERVES 4

⅔ CUP PIMMS

¾ CUP LEMONADE

¾ CUP GINGER ALE

A SQUEEZE OF LEMON

5 LEAVES OF GELATIN

1 CUP ASSORTED FRUIT — USE WHAT YOU CAN GET!

CHOPPED CUCUMBER

FRESH MINT TO GARNISH

Sex on the beach jelly

Roll up the sleeves of your pastel blazer! Snap on your sunglasses! Here's a jelly to spirit you instantly to a yacht off the Florida Keys. An exotic Sex on the Beach jelly will have guests describing your hosting technique to neighbors for weeks to come. Don't forget to turn on Duran Duran's *Rio*. Here's to sunsets, seagulls and palm trees!

ENOUGH FOR 6 WOBBLY COCKTAILS

GENEROUS ¾ CUP VODKA

SCANT ½ CUP PEACH SCHNAPPS

GENEROUS ¾ CUP CRANBERRY JUICE

GENEROUS ¾ CUP ORANGE JUICE

5 LEAVES OF GELATIN

FLESH OF 2 ORANGES, FINELY DICED

6 MARTINI GLASSES

6 COCKTAIL UMBRELLAS

CANDIED CHERRIES

In a pitcher, combine the vodka, schnapps, cranberry juice and orange juice.

Cut up the gelatin into thumb-size pieces and place in a heatproof bowl. Pour over enough of the cocktail mixture to cover and allow to soften for 10 minutes.

Meanwhile, bring a small pan of water to a simmer. Place the softened bowl of gelatin on top of the simmering water and stir occasionally until dissolved. This will take about 10 minutes.

While you are waiting, dice the orange flesh and divide among the cocktail glasses. Once the gelatin has entirely melted, mix with the remainder of the cocktail mixture and pour through a sieve into the glasses. Refrigerate to set.

Garnish with the cocktail umbrellas and some candied cherries before serving.

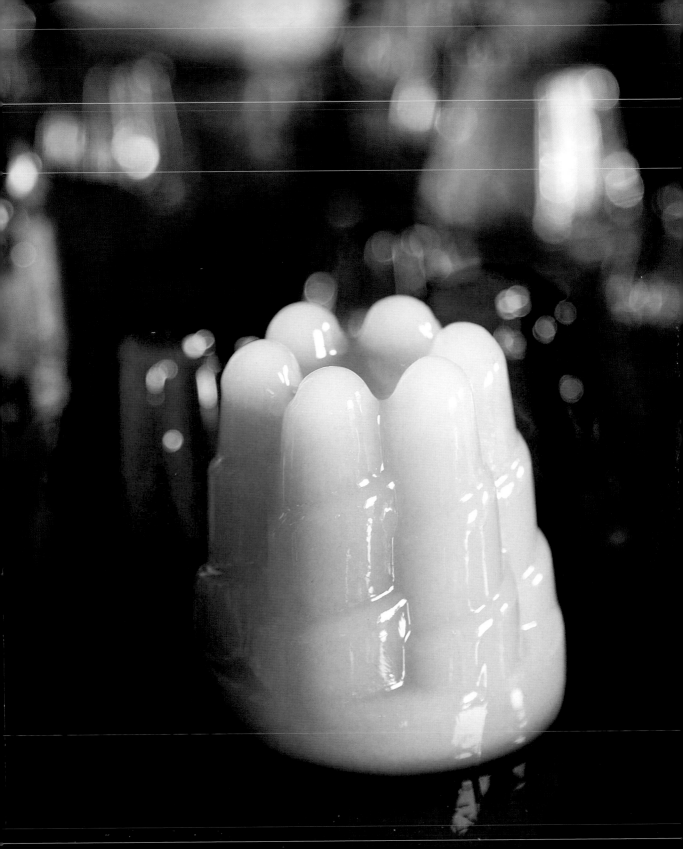

WEIRD & WONDERFUL

FUNERAL JELLY

This jelly is our take on funeral cakes, a long forgotten element of the funeral ceremony. In the past, funeral cakes – which were much like shortbread – were served with a glass of ale or Madeira after the interment. Two young women called "servers" distributed the cakes, and it was these women who walked at the head of the funeral procession. The cakes were traditionally wrapped in black crepe paper and molded to depict motifs such as skulls, hearts and roses.

We initially became interested in funeral cakes because they are a prime example of a molded food as well as being thrillingly macabre. Original funeral molds were made in metal, wood and ceramic, and motifs included the three plumes that decorate hearses; roosters, symbolizing resurrection; and Masonic symbols.

After a bit of research, we let things lie until we were asked to make a jelly for someone's funeral! Wow! It seemed like a good opportunity to revive the

custom of funeral cakes but in a magical jellied format. In retrospect, it makes sense. We produce vast amounts of jelly for jaded wedding guests, so it's understandable that grieving families want in on the action. After all, funerals and weddings are both celebrations of life.

The trick was to create a recipe and design a mold that were both in keeping with the tone of the ceremony. We settled on a simple pyramid mold, referencing the grandest tombs of all time. A black cherry and prosecco jelly complimented the somber yet celebratory occasion, and is lent extra panache by the 24-karat-gold tip.

After debuting the funeral jelly at the private event, we looked for an opportunity to launch a funeral jelly service to the general public. One presented itself with the global wave of grief around Michael Jackson's death. London restaurant Bistrotheque bodly put the jelly on the menu for the day of Michael Jackson's funeral, and diners were served quivering pyramids by waiters wearing a single white glove.

BLACK CHERRY & PROSECCO FUNERAL JELLY

It is hoped that the Funeral Jelly will act as powerful *memento mori* to inspire eaters to live life to the fullest. At the end of some Egyptian feasts, a small model of a mummified corpse was passed around before wine was served, to prompt the feasters to seize the day. *Carpe diem!*

FOR 10 SMALL JELLIES

FOR THE GOLDEN TIPS,
SEE PP.74—75.

SCANT 1LB BLACK CHERRIES

¼ CUP SUGAR

1½ CUPS PROSECCO

JUICE OF ½ LEMON

5 LEAVES OF GELATIN

Begin by making your golden tips (see instructions on pp.74—75). Ensure they have time to fully set while you embark on the rest of the recipe.

Start by adding the black cherries to a small saucepan with the sugar and a scant ½ cup of the prosecco. Cook covered over a low heat until the cherries are tender — up to 45 minutes. Pass the softened cherries and juice through a sieve lined with cheesecloth placed over a large measuring cup. Let gravity do the work — we want the juice to be extra smooth.

Once the black cherry juice has run through into the measuring cup, add the rest of the prosecco and lemon juice. You need 2 generous cups of liquid, so add more prosecco if necessary.

Use some of this liquid to cover your chopped gelatin in a bowl. Allow the gelatin to soften for 5 minutes. Bring a pan of water to a boil and place the bowl of softened gelatin on top of the pan. Once the gelatin has melted, add half of the cherry mixture at the last minute, then strain the gelatin mixture back into the measuring cup, stirring all the time.

Now you are ready to pour the black cherry jelly into the mold on top of the gold layer. Before you do so, make sure the gold layer is fully set. It's worth making sure that the cherry mix has cooled to room temperature too. If it is poured hot, you risk melting some of the gold mixture, and gold leaf will float around the rest of the jelly, which won't look at all elegant. Lower the temperature by stirring the mixture over ice. Alternatively, pour the jelly out onto a tray and the temperature will drop rapidly.

Finish setting the jelly in the refrigerator for a couple of hours.

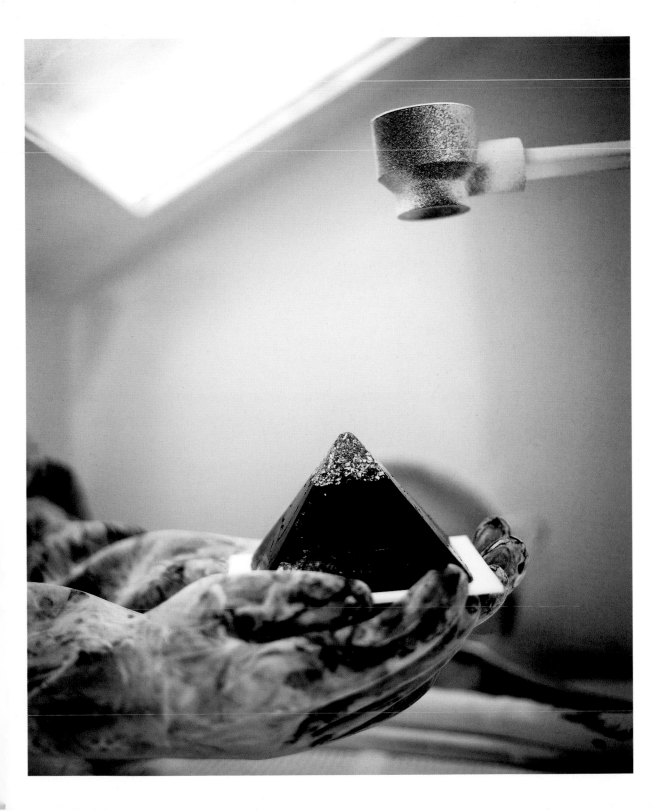

HIPPOCRAS

There is real scope to bring back the jelly as a Christmas dessert and alternative to heavy Christmas puddings. Stomachs need to be respected — indeed, the Victorians often referred to them as amiable gentlemen — and a light jelly makes a much more manageable alternative. We'll demonstrate that you can ditch the Christmas pudding but lose none of the traditions.

For this jelly, we use a recipe once enjoyed by Henry VIII and which the notorious serial killer Gilles de Rais called "Jelly Hippocras." Hippocras is a medieval drink that is similar to mulled wine, infused with spices and sugar, but it was invariably served at room temperature. As with traditional Christmas pudding, it's important that 13 ingredients are used to represent Jesus and his disciples. Interestingly, Christmas puddings were banned by the Puritans in 1664 for being lewd. If they had seen the wobble on this Christmas pudding, they'd have been even more shocked.

The golden age of jelly and the origins of modern Christmas both come from the same period — the Victorians are responsible for both. Christmas trees were not popularized in the United Kingdom until 1848, when the Royal Family were pictured standing in front of one. At this time, jelly was considered a fine centerpiece and was often laid along the table for the entirety of the meal.

Sadly, jelly no longer takes center stage at Christmas, though it continues to play an important supporting role. We're all familiar with cranberry and red-currant jelly. Jams and preserves, close relatives to jelly, come into their own at this time of year, when fresh fruit is in short supply.

The Victorians set lots of small keepsakes within their Christmas puddings, which were used to foretell the future. If you set items in the jelly, you can do the same. If you discover a ring, legend has it the next year will bring true love; coins bring wealth; and thimbles are the booby prize. If you get a thimble in your pudding, you'll remain single forever!

CONTINUES ON PAGE 121 >

JOLLY OLD CHRISTMAS.

HIPPOCRAS CHRISTMAS PUDDING JELLY

Hippocras improves with resting, but if you don't tend to plan meals a month in advance it will still be just fine. This recipe gives you more than you will need for a Christmas pudding for four, so you can serve the rest at cocktail parties around the festive period.

All you have to do is add all the ingredients for the hippocras to a large stock pot and heat gently for 1 hour. At this point, it can be strained and stored in sterilized bottles as necessary. Traditionally, the wine would steep in the spices for a week or more before being strained.

TO MAKE THE CHRISTMAS PUDDING JELLY

Cut the leaf gelatin into a heatproof bowl with a pair of scissors. Add a scant ½ cup of hippocras to cover the gelatin.

Leave the gelatin to soften for 10 minutes. Bring a pan of water to a boil and place the bowl of softened gelatin on top of the pan. Once the gelatin has totally melted, add the rest of the hippocras to the mixture before passing the entire contents through a sieve and back into a bowl.

Place the bowl with the cooling jelly over a larger bowl filled with ice. Now stir until the mixture starts to thicken. At this point, you can add the raisins and candied peel. (In the U.K., a ring, small coin, or thimble is also added, but since they are choking hazards this is not recommended.) You need to stir the jelly to the point that you can get all your objects evenly distributed but not so much that the jelly is excessively lumpy. It still has to be able to fill all the contours of your mold (or pudding basin). When the jelly is just right, encourage it into a mold and place in the refrigerator to finish setting.

All that's left now is to unmold the jelly and discover who is going to be unlucky in love for the rest of their life. If you're going all-out, garnish the jelly with holly and pour over 1 tablespoon of rum before igniting it.

For the Hippocras

3 BOTTLES RED WINE

1 CUP SUPERFINE SUGAR

1 CINNAMON STICK

2 TSP GROUND GINGER

1 TSP GRATED NUTMEG

1 TSP CLOVES

1 TSP CRUSHED CARDAMOM SEEDS

For the Jelly

5 LEAVES OF GELATIN

GENEROUS 2 CUPS HIPPOCRAS

2 TSP RAISINS

2 TSP CANDIED CITRUS PEEL

GLOW IN THE DARK JELLY

With jelly, half the fun lies in the spectacle. People always enjoy the wobble, but that's to be expected. No one is surprised by a wobbly jelly. To really bowl them over, you have to sex it up a lot. One way of doing this is to make it glow in the dark.

In the summer of 2009, we were commissioned to create the most outlandish menu imaginable to be served on a Pullman train carriage touring the country. The event was organized by Hendrick's Gin, and curious visitors were plied with fine alcohol. The most interesting visitors were invited to a banquet hosted in the carriage each evening, which they were assured would be the most peculiar meal of their life.

We wanted to use the gin as part of a jelly that took people by surprise and ambushed their senses. Weird-tasting jelly would be too obvious — and not nice! So visual trickery was the key.

The previous year we had worked with Dr. Andrea Sella, an explosives expert at University College London, developing glow in the dark jelly. We decided to use the techniques developed in his laboratory for maximum impact on the carriage. The dinner guests went wild!

To make the jelly glow in the dark, food-safe quinine is included as an ingredient and the jelly is served in an area where UV black lights cause them to fluoresce. The invisible ultraviolet light from the black lights is absorbed by the quinine, which then re-emits bluish light at the edge of the visible spectrum, making the jelly appear to glow in the dark.

Dr. Sella explains the phenomenon like this:

Fluorescence is one of those truly magical atomic phenomena — an optical illusion that makes things look brighter than they are, making it central not only to safety equipment but also to detergents and cleaning agents to give that "whiter than white" look. All manner of materials fluoresce. The quinine molecule itself is a natural product from the bark of the South American Cinchona tree, [which] has been added to drinks for over a century. One of the first antimalarial molecules, it began to be used by the British in India as a cure for fevers. The drug could be made more palatable by judicious addition of sugar and alcohol. Nowadays, the malaria parasite is resistant to quinine, but the molecule's bitterness adds a pleasant "bite" to the flavor of many soft drinks and mixers. And the blue glow is a delightful effect that adds ambience to pubs and clubs. But if you don't like the glow there's a simple way to switch it off — simply toss a pinch of salt into your cocktail and kill the effect in an instant.

To be really effective, you need total darkness save for the UV light. We were running the banquets on summer nights in a train carriage with no blinds, so there was a good deal of ambient light well into the evening. We hid a UV light underneath the dining table in the carriage. When it came to the dessert course, guests were encouraged to hold their plates in the relative darkness under the table to see the glow. The jellies sprang into vivid glowing colors. Most peculiar was not the glowing jelly but watching all the guests holding their plates under the table!

We have used rose water and gin to create our glow in the dark cocktail. All that remains is for you to get a UV black light from your local hardware or home renovation store and the fun begins...

GIN 'N' ROSES JELLY

For the Jelly

GENEROUS ⅔ CUP GIN

1½ CUPS TONIC WATER

A SPLASH OF ROSE WATER

5 LEAVES OF GELATIN

For the Glow

UV BLACK LIGHT

Combine the gin, tonic water, and rose water in a pitcher or large measuring cup and set aside. Cut the gelatin into fine pieces and place in a heatproof bowl with enough of the gin and tonic mix to submerse. Leave until soft. When the gelatin has softened, place it over a pan of simmering water to melt. Then add the remainder of the gin and tonic. Pour through a sieve and back into the pitcher or large measuring cup. Now fill your mold.

Unmold the jelly by briefly immersing in a bowl of hot water and inverting over your chosen plates. For maximum effect, turn off all lights to achieve total darkness. Switch on your black light and serve the glowing jelly to thrilled diners.

WHY DOES THE JELLY GLOW?

The quinine in the tonic water is UV-active. When the black light is switched on, it will fluoresce beautifully.

CUCUMBER ICE CREAM

2 CUCUMBERS

GENEROUS ¾ CUP WATER

1½ CUPS SUPERFINE SUGAR

2½ CUPS HEAVY CREAM

SCANT ¼ CUP GIN

JUICE OF 1 LARGE LEMON

3 DROPS OF BERGAMOT OIL

We serve this jelly with cucumber ice cream. Harry adapted the recipe from *Mrs. Marshall's Book on Ices.* It's surprisingly tasty.

Peel and deseed the cucumbers. Chop them finely and place in a saucepan with the water and sugar. Cook gently until the cucumbers are tender. This will take about 45 minutes. Strain them and place in a pitcher or large measuring cup. Bash them to a purée using the end of a rolling pin. Pass the purée through a fine sieve and add the heavy cream, gin, lemon juice and bergamot oil. Stir thoroughly and pour into an ice-cream machine to freeze. The semifrozen mixture can be spooned into any mold and placed in the feezer to firm up. To unmold, dip briefly in cold water. It should slide out. It's best to let it soften for 10 minutes before serving.

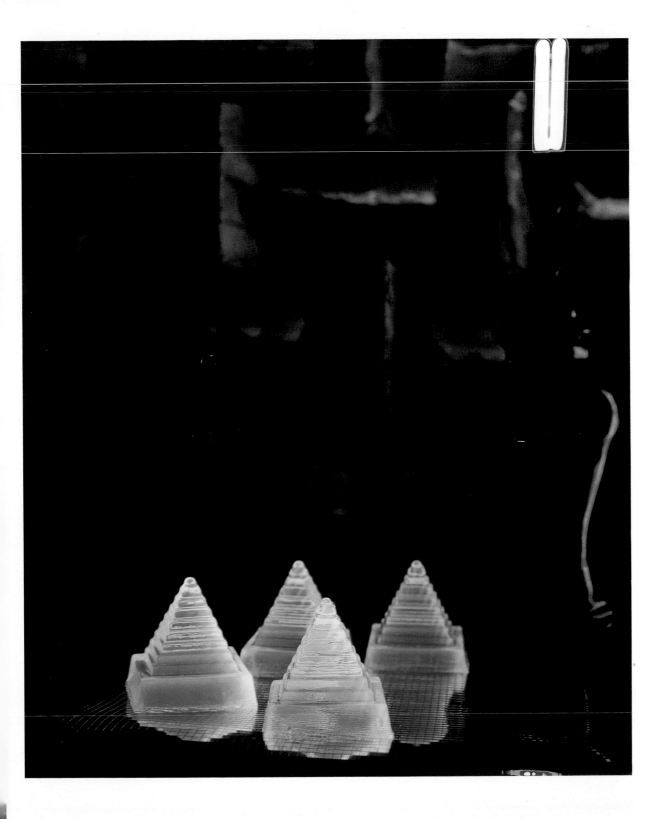

BLACK FOOD

Don't you think it's appropriate that the most expensive items are
black? THE COOK, THE THIEF, HIS WIFE AND HER LOVER

Black is beautiful and black food has provided the basis for some of the most
memorable literary and historic meals. In Huysman's *Against Nature*, the
hero Des Esseintes hosts a feast:

The dining room, draped in black, opened out onto a garden
metamorphosed for the occasion, the paths being strewn with
charcoal, the ornamental pond edged with black basalt and filled
with ink, and the shrubberies replanted with cypresses and pines.
The dinner itself was served on a black cloth adorned with baskets
of violets and scabious; a candelabrum shed an eerie green light over
the table and tapers flickered in the chandeliers.

While a hidden orchestra played funeral marches, the guests were
waited on by naked negresses wearing only slippers and stockings in
cloth of silver embroiderd with tears.

Dining off black-bordered plates, the company had enjoyed turtle
soup, Russian rye bread, ripe olives from Turkey, caviar, mullet
botargo, black puddings from Frankfurt, game served in sauce the
color of liquorices and boot-polish, truffle jellies, chocolate creams,
plum-puddings, nectarines, pears in grape-juice syrup, mulberries,
and black-heart cherries. From dark-tinted glasses they had drunk
the wines of Limagne and Roussillon, of Tenedos, Valdepenas, and
Oporto. And after coffee and walnut cordial, they had rounded off
the evening with kvass, porter and stout.

On the invitations, which were similar to those sent out before more
solemn obsequies, this dinner was described as a funeral banquet in
memory of the host's virility, lately but only temporarily deceased.

This literary meal was based on an earlier banquet that had caused a scandal in Parisian high society. In 1783, Grimond de La Reynière, seen by many as the first restaurant critic, hosted a black banquet with invitations so extraordinary that Louis XVI is said to have aquired one to frame. Bordered in black to resemble funeral notices, these were sent to 300 guests, although only 22 were to dine: following the protocol of the time, the rest were to observe the festivities.

There's also a well documented Renaissance black, or hell, banquet hosted in 1511 by dining group The Company of the Trowel. On arrival, guests were invited by Pluto to join him in the Underworld for his wedding feast to Proserpina. Entering through the gaping mouth of Hades, which was hinged to open and close for each couple in turn, guests found themselves in a circular room gloomily lit by one small candle. A hideous devil with pitchfork showed them to their places at a black draped table, while their host declaimed that the torments of Hell would be suspended for the time being in honor of his wedding. About the walls of the room were pictured the "holes" of the damned, their varying tortures periodically revealed by "flames" that flared up beneath them.

The food served seemed repulsive — serpents, lizards, toads, newts, spiders, frogs, scorpions and the like. Inside these deceptive exteriors, though, delicious tidbits were hidden. The dishes were served on a fire shovel, while wine was poured by a "devil" from a rhyton, a drinking vessel in the shape of an animal's head. Skeleton bones made of sugar and marzipan formed the dessert course.

This weight of precedent is inspirational. We teamed up with party planner Fiona Leahy and Michael Cirino of *a razor, a shiny knife* to create our own monochromatic meal. Michael created an eight-course meal, where all the dishes were black; we built black licorice jello ziggurats; and Fiona created the most spectacular setting.

LICORICE JELLY

You can buy licorice sticks from health food stores. The sticks are very brittle and, arguably, inedible. However, when soaked they render an unbelievably sweet and dark licorice water. It is this licorice water that is going to be used to flavor the jelly.

Break the licorice up into ½-in long pieces and place in a large measuring cup. Add about ⅔ cup of water, or certainly enough so that the sticks are covered. Stir with a fork from time to time. It will take about 2 hours for the licorice to dissolve. To speed up the process, you can chop the sticks up smaller to begin with.

The liquid will now be a deep black color, highly flavored and very sweet. Licorice contains a naturally occurring sweetner called glycyrrhizin, which can be 50 times sweeter than sugar, so you don't need to add any sugar to the jello.

Using water, dilute the licorice water to taste. If you want to go for a strong flavor, add more water until you have a generous 2 cups.

Cut the leaves of gelatin into a few pieces and place in a heatproof bowl. Add a few tablespoons of the licorice-water mixture so that the gelatin is just covered. Let the gelatin soften for 10 minutes while you bring a small pan of water to a simmer. Place the bowl of softened gelatin over the simmering water and leave until totally melted. Add the remainder of the licorice-water mixture to the melted gelatin and stir to combine.

Pour through a strainer into a pitcher or back into the large measuring cup and then carefully fill your mold. Refrigerate until set.

1 STICK OF LICORICE

⅔ CUP WATER

5 LEAVES OF GELATIN

BACON COLA JELLIES

Fat-washing may sound disgusting. But it does let you infuse various liquids with the flavor of melted fat – and if done properly does not leave a greasy taste or texture. Some of the top bars and restaurants are using the technique to create unusal beverages like buttered rums. And we use it to make Bacon Cola Jelly. You can use the technique to impress your friends and scare vegetarians.

As a fizzy drink is used in this jelly, there is a techniqe (developed by food scientist Len Fisher and used by leading chef Heston Blumenthal) to make the jelly extra fizzy. The trick is to cool the jelly rapidly and to ensure that the cola is at it's fizziest when added to the mix.

For the Fat-washed Vodka

6 SLICES OF SMOKED BACON

GENEROUS ¾ CUP VODKA

For the Jelly

5 LEAVES OF GELATIN

GENEROUS ¾ CUP BACON VODKA

SQUEEZE OF LEMON

1¼ CUPS CHILLED COLA

BACON VODKA

Fry the bacon and let it cool on paper towel, then add it to the vodka in a sealed plastic container. Place the container in a dark cupboard for about 2 weeks, or until you get bored. Move the container to the freezer. The fat will freeze, but the vodka will not. Filter the bacon vodka through coffee filters. This will keep indefinitely.

EXTRA FIZZY JELLIES

Place four glasses in the freezer to cool down.

Cut the gelatin into a heatproof bowl and add half the bacon vodka. Leave the gelatin to soften for 10 minutes. Add the lemon juice.

Bring a pan of water to a boil and place the bowl of softened gelatin on top. Once the gelatin has melted, add the remainder of the vodka and stir. Sieve into a pitcher. Divide equally between the four frozen glasses.

Open the cola and quick as a flash divide this among the four glasses. Place all the glasses back in the freezer for 20 minutes – and no longer. It's important that your jelly does not freeze, or it will be ruined.

Transfer the jellies to the refrigerator to set for around 6 hours. Using this technique will make for super-fizzy jelly.

FLAMING JELLY

This is less of a recipe and more of an instructional. You can turn any jelly into a flaming jelly!

We looked at loads of different ways of doing this, using some "serious" chemicals and speaking to some top scientists. We developed the methods using complex setting techinques and some strange chemicals; they worked pretty effectively. What works even more effectively, though, is the simplest method. Pour over-proof spirit over your jelly and torch it. The more potent the spirit, the better it will burn. When Sam does this, he uses a 151% proof spirit. Alcohol burns with a low-temperature flame, so the jelly won't melt too much before the alcohol burns off and the flames die down.

Weirdly, the less explanation you give, the more people will think you are doing something terribly clever. Some aspects of cooking are a bit like doing a magic trick. When you know how it's done, it seems obvious and tired. When you don't know the method, it appears to be a miracle.

The most memorable time setting fire to jelly was at the Oxford Symposium on Food and Cookery. Sam and his brother created a banquet table for a Samuel Pepys memorial meal cooked by Fergus Henderson (Pepys' 17th-century diary offers a first-hand account of the Fire of London.) They made the Great Fire of London in jelly with a huge centerpiece of the old St. Paul's Cathedral surrounded by hundreds of jelly houses. When the diners had gathered, the jelly was spectacularly set alight. Sam's brother was holding a large burning tray of jelly and was getting seriously scorched. But every time he cried out for someone to bring a towel to beat out the flames, the crowd cheered more — they thought it was part of the act! He managed to carry it off, but the situation was pretty intense.

Aphrodisiac Jelly

The best way to get someone into bed is to touch their most sensitive organ – the belly!

Over the course of history, pretty much every vaguely exotic ingredient has been seen as an aphrodisiac. Vanilla, oysters and bananas all look rude, and have been credited with mysterious powers of arousal. There's little to substantiate their claims.

What works is extravagance and alcohol. If the food looks and tastes expensive and combines a knockout punch, you're getting there. Flowers also help. This recipe sexes-up our wedding jelly formula to make it go with a bang. When we served it at the School of Life's Sunday morning sermon on seduction, one man exposed himself. We're not sure how seductive this was, but it goes to show that the recipe makes an impact.

CHAMPAGNE, ROSE & STRAWBERRY JELLY

Use 1 leaf of gelatin, the gold, and 3½ tablespoons of the Champagne to make a gold and Champagne suspension, following the technique on p.74–75. Set this as the first layer of your jelly in the mold.

Meanwhile, cut the rest of the leaf gelatin into a heatproof bowl with a pair of scissors. Add enough Champagne to cover (about a scant ½ cup). Leave the gelatin to soften for 10 minutes.

Bring a pan of water to a boil and place the bowl of softened gelatin on top of the pan of boiling water. Once the gelatin has totally melted, stir in the sugar until it has dissolved and add another scant ½ cup of Champagne to the mixture.

Combine the melted gelatin mixture with the rest of the Champagne by pouring it through a sieve and into a large measuring cup; this will also remove any unmelted lumps. Add the rose extract to the mixture. Squeeze the lemon through the sieve too. Add more Champagne until you have a generous 2 cups.

Place the washed fruit into the bottom of the mold and pour in about ⅓ of the jelly mixture. Put the mold in the refrigerator for the jelly to set. Leave until set enough so the fruit seems safely embedded (about 2 hours), then pour over the rest of the jelly mixture and return to the refrigerator.

If you don't want to set the fruit in the mold first, simply add everything to the mold at once. Doing a double set, however, ensures that the fruit floats elegantly in the unmolded jelly rather than sinking to the bottom.

FOR GENEROUS 2 CUPS, SERVES 4

5 LEAVES OF GELATIN

5 LEAVES OF GOLD LEAF

SCANT 2 CUPS CHAMPAGNE OR SPARKLING WINE

SCANT ¼ CUP SUPERFINE SUGAR

4 TSP ROSE EXTRACT

A SQUEEZE OF LEMON JUICE

A FEW STRAWBERRIES

SUN-COFFEE JELLY

You can make this jelly using coffee in the regular way, but it won't have the same pizzazz. Sun-infusing coffee or tea brings out a completely different flavor profile. Most importantly, more caffeine is extracted, which means you can make a jelly that's like rocket fuel.

FOR THE INFUSION

For the Infusion

GENEROUS 2 CUPS WATER

SCANT ½ CUP DARK-ROASTED COFFEE AT A COARSE GRIND

1 SMALL CINAMMON STICK

Sam likes to use a dark-roasted coffee, because it has a stronger flavor profile, which means the coffee taste transfers more effectively. You also get a richer color.

Place the water and coffee in a glass jar with a lid. Seal the jar and then give it a shake. Put the jar outside where the sun will strike it and try to shake vigorously every now and again. Leave for two to three days. Remove the cinammon stick and then pour through coffee filter paper to remove the grinds.

FOR THE JELLY

For the Jelly

SCANT 2 CUPS SUN-INFUSED COFFEE

SCANT ¼ CUP SUGAR SYRUP

1 DROP VANILLA EXTRACT

5 LEAVES OF GELATIN

Combine the sun-infused coffee, sugar syrup and vanilla extract in a pitcher or large measuring cup.

Cut the leaf gelatin into a heatproof bowl and add enough of the coffee mixture to cover. Leave the gelatin to soften for 10 minutes. Bring a pan of water to a boil and place the bowl of softened gelatin on top of the pan.

Once the gelatin has totally melted, add some of the remaining coffee mixture to the bowl. Stir and then pour everything through a sieve into the pitcher or measuring cup.

Pour this mixture into a mold and place in the refrigerator to set.

APPENDIX

GELLING AGENTS

There are better things to do in life than read a chapter about gels. But if you are really interested, here's what we know:

GELATIN

Gelatin is the ultimate gelling agent. Gelatin jelly is wonderful to look at, glistens beautifully and has a marvelous wobble. It has a suppleness and texture that makes gelatin jelly a joy to eat. The melting point is below body temperature, which means it melts in the mouth.

You will need to come to terms with the fact that gelatin is derived from animals. In Europe and North America, gelatin is mostly derived from pigskin, though it is sometimes made from cowskin or from bone. This does seem a bit brutal but we like to think that these by-products of industrial meat production would go to waste if they weren't turned into fine jellies.

Now for the chemistry bit. Gelatin comes from the collagen proteins extracted (via acid baths) from animal skin. When heated, the collagen's triple helix structure uncoils and dissolves in the water. As it cools below the melting temperature of gelatin (around body temperature), the collagen naturally tries to reorganize itself into its original triple helix. However, it does not attain this original structure because adjacent collagen helixes randomly bind to one another to form a net of gelatin molecules. At a concentration of about one per cent, this net traps the liquid in its interstices, stopping movement and turning the solution into a gel. If you want even more of this sort of thing look at *McGee on Food and Cooking* or the *Big Fat Duck Cookbook* – they're our first port of call when we need to get scientific!

Using higher concentrations of gelatin will give you a stronger jelly. It will be less fragile and won't melt as fast outside the refrigerator. On the other hand, if you have a jelly that has too high a concentration, it will wobble less and become rubbery (and will even bounce when dropped). In this book, we have calibrated the gel strength for good eating jellies.

Gelatin comes in a number of differet forms. You can buy powdered gelatin and leaf gelatin in grades ranging from bronze to platinum. We like to use high grade leaf gelatin, which gives a clearer jelly without the yellowish tinge and piggy smell of the lower grades. Lower grade gelatin and powdered gelatin is, of course, cheaper. It is useful for making jellies to look at rather than eat.

USING POWDERED GELATIN

Make up the mixture that you want to gel and add it to a small saucepan. Sprinkle the gelatin on top and let it soften for 10 minutes or so. Then place the pan on a low heat and stir the mixture constantly until all the gelatin has been incorporated. Check by splashing a little up the side of the pan and look to see if any gelatin remains. Whatever you do, don't let the mixture boil — it only takes a minute to melt the gelatin, so it's worth giving it your undivided attention. Just to make sure you've melted everything, pass through a sieve before filling your mold.

There are a number of other factors that will increase and decrease your gel strength. Adjust the concentration of gelatin accordingly:

- the longer you leave a jelly in the refrigerator, the stronger it gets

- acids, such as lemon juice, make a weaker jelly

- alcohol above 45% proof stops gelatin from setting

- some fruit like kiwi fruit and pineapples have protein-digesting enzymes that will stop a jelly from setting. For instructions on how to counter this, see p.50.

- milk-based jelly sets firmer

- the more slowly you let the temperature of the jelly drop, the more effectively the gelatin network can organize, and so the greater the strength of the gel

A vegetarian gelling agent as good as gelatin remains the holy grail of food scientists. The person that cracks it will be rich. Here is a non-meaty gelling agent:

AGAR AGAR

Agar agar is a vegetarian gel extracted from a number of red seaweeds. It is commonly used in the study of microbiology, but you can use it to make hot jellies. Agar is commonly used in Asia to make fruit jelly. If it's not stocked in your local supermarket, head across to a Japanese or Chinese grocery store.

To make an agar jelly, you won't need as high a concerntration as with gelatin – between 0.5% and 1.5% of the final volume of the gel. First soak the agar in cold water, then heat it to a boil to fully dissolve it. Once you have combined the agar with the other ingredients and strained the mixture, it will set at around 100°F (38°C). You won't even need to put it in the refrigerator. After an agar gel has set, it won't remelt until it is heated beyond 185°F (85°C). You can use this property to make hot jellies. We sometimes use agar to make a hot apple crumble jelly – though it's not especially nice!

The problem with agar jellies is that they lack the glorious texture and mouthfeel of gelatin jellies. Agar jellies won't wobble as well, are more crumbly, look slightly opaque and most importantly, don't melt in the mouth. Due to the higher melting point, they are also impossible to unmold.

Canny cooks can combine weak gelatin gels with agar gels to enjoy the benefits of both gelling agents. So you can get a jelly that wobbles and has a decent texture (from the gelatin) but is more stable up until you serve it (thanks to the agar).

Using ceramic
& glass molds

Not all jelly molds are made of copper, and it's a good bet that you've got some ceramic or glass molds sitting around. But, as many will testify, they can be impossible to unmold. Both glass and ceramic are poor conductors of heat, so you can't rely on putting them in a basin of hot water to loosen the jelly. By the time the last part of the surface has melted, there's a chance that half the jelly has melted too.

Food historian Ivan Day discovered that the traditional way of using these molds was to first line them with a thin layer of tallow (mutton fat). The tallow was brushed onto the inside of the mold and the jelly carefully poured in. It was vital that the jelly was relatively cool so as not to melt the tallow. Fortunately, Ivan doesn't suggest that you track down some rendered mutton fat but instead use its modern equivalent, vegetable shortening, which is available in all supermarkets.

TO PREPARE THE MOLD

Use a pastry brush to apply a thin film of vegetable shortening onto the inside of the mold, making sure that you continue right up to the rim. Pour the cool jelly in and refrigerate until set.

TO UNMOLD THE JELLY

Firstly gently push down around the perimeter of the jelly using your fingers so that the jelly pulls away from the mold. Then, turning the jelly on its side, give it a good shake: if you hear it making slapping noises, you know that it is ready to be turned out. If it won't perform a rude wobble solo for you, try to get some air into the mold by carefully putting a finger between the mold and the jelly – crude but it works. It does take some practice, but the results are worth it.

If you are having difficulty unmolding from thick-gauge plastic molds, the above method will work wonders on them too.

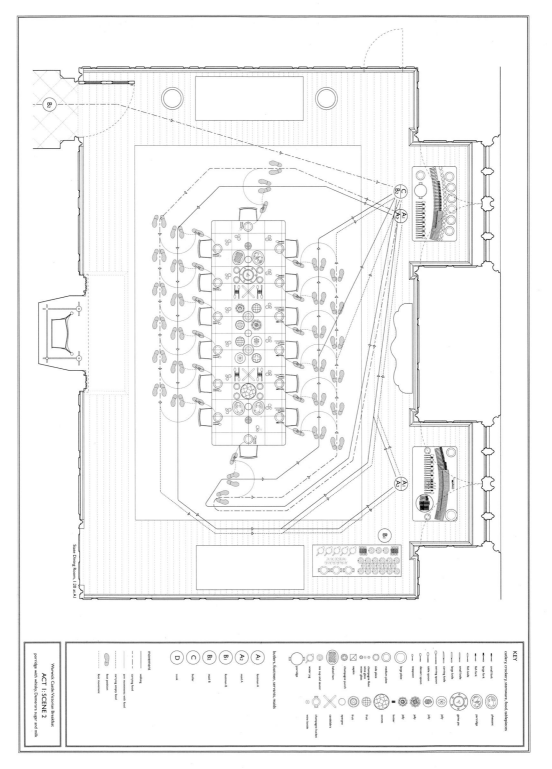

State Dining Room, 1:20 at A1

Warwick Castle:Victorian Breakfast
ACT 1 1:SCENE 2
porridge with whisky, Demerara sugar and milk

KEY
cutlery, crockery, stemware, food, tablepieces

butlers, footmen, servants, maids

movement

EVENTS

Victorian Breakfast *Warwick Castle* December 2007

Warwick Castle commissioned us to create a full-blown, 12-course Victorian breakfast. We got stuck into some serious research and discovered that a breakfast of similar magnitude had been served to Queen Victoria on a train. Drawing on this for inspiration, we wrote our menu.

It was huge. A single person's meal clocked in at more than 4,000 calories. Just one of the courses was a full English breakfast; another was a dish called scotch woodcock, basically a sexed-up version of scrambled eggs, using only yolks and double cream, and served with anchovies.

Each guest needed a battery of cutlery to get through the meal, so the table had to be reset three times. To add to the difficulties, the food was coming out of three separate kitchens. Harry drew up architectural drawings showing table setting and resetting, food production flows and serving choreography for each of the 12 courses. It got us through.

An edge of surrealism was added by the life size waxwork of Queen Victoria standing at the side of the dining room, and the organ music from the fairground outside.

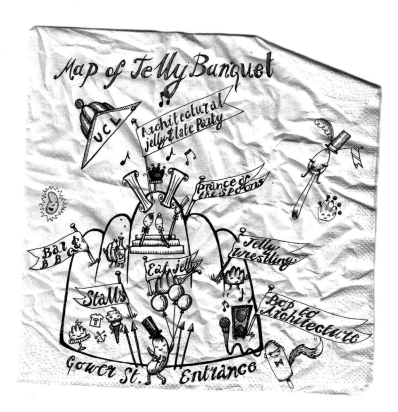

To cement the link between jelly and architecture, we put on an Architectural Jelly Banquet in the mighty Quad of University College, London (UCL). In the days before the event, we created a jelly design competition, which attracted entries from some of the world's leading architects, including Rogers Stirk Harbour + Partners, Lord Foster and Will Alsop. In total, more than a hundred designs were submitted from as far afield as Brazil and the United States.

For the event, we lit the buildings of UCL's Neo-Classical Quad to look like jellies and pumped the space full of the smell of strawberries. It was like stepping inside a vast jelly. More than 2,000 people came to look at the jelly designs, eat jelly and party. The centerpiece was a 46-foot long self-wobbling jelly table with hundreds of illuminated jellies. It looked spectacular. A waggle engine strapped to the bottom of the table created a nonstop wobbling effect.

Choreographed dancers performed with giant spoons against a soundscape by Douglas Murphey made from sampling jellies wobbling. He used UCL's anechoic chamber — a special room lined with sound absorbing materials, to record the sound of jelly wobbling. The sonic wobble was captured in two ways: by carefully recording the results of gentle coaxing and by expressing the wobble frequency as physically powerful bass tones. It sounded rude. You can listen for yourself on YouTube.

Heston Blumenthal popped down to present the prize of ultimate jelly architect to Tonkin Liu. At 11p.m., the exhibition wound up and the party began with jelly wrestling and a huge food fight.

Scratch 'n' Sniff Cinema *ICA/Jotta Craft Fair* February 2009

Making Peter Greenaway's *The Cook, The Thief, His Wife and Her Lover* an even more visceral experience is a challenge. For a Valentine's Day screening, we created aromas including "rotting meat" and "dusty books" to capture the scent of key moments of the movie. These aromas were micro-encapsulated and printed onto special scratch 'n' sniff cards given to the audience to scratch along to the production.

During an extended intermission, they got stuck into a cinema food concession that had been possessed by the movie. The popcorn machine held a naked body, hotdogs were enrobed with 24-karat gold, and the pick 'n' mix featured flashing hard candies, and roll-your-own candy tobacco.

Brilliantly, we were able to corner Peter Greenaway at the ICA the week before. He kindly let us record an interview to introduce the movie. While we were talking, he let slip what he would cook to seduce a woman: crocodile!

Because the printing on the scratch 'n' sniff cards was so expensive, we had to run three consecutive screenings to break even. We were haunted by the movie's soundtrack for weeks afterward from listening to it nonstop.

So many people turned up to the final screening that we had to beg bar stools from the pub next door and borrow chairs from the offices across the road to seat everyone.

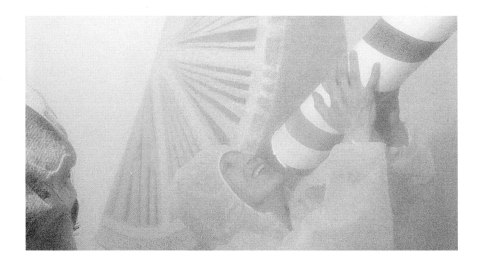

Alcoholic Architecture *Newburgh Quarter, London* April 2009

Buildings can be transformed into breathable beverages by filling them with a cocktail fog. At the Alcoholic Architecture event Bompas & Parr created a walk-in cloud of breathable cocktail.

In the temporary bar, visitors donned protective suits and stepped into a mist of vaporized gin and tonic, which they imbibed through inhaling. Doctors were our mixologists for the event, performing a complex series of calculations to calibrate the ratio of alcohol to mixer. It was important that visitors were able to walk out of the installation and not crawl out on their hands and knees!

Stepping inside the cloud was strange and disorienting. If your friend was three feet away, you weren't able to see them because there was so much Hendrick's Gin and tonic in the air between you.

Vaporizing the cocktail seemed to heighten the flavor for an ultra-intense G&T experience. Visitors from the Institute of Food Research thought that breathing in different ways let them taste the different botanicals in the gin. All the while, the alcohol was being absorbed via the lungs and even the eyeballs.

Architectural Punch Bowl *33 Portland Place, London* December 2009

For the Architectural Punch Bowl we worked with Courvoisier to explode cocktails to the grandest size – the scale of buildings. After a six-month research project with UCL we flooded 33 Portland Place with more than four tons of punch; enough for 25,000 people. The Punch Bowl was so large that engineers Arup had to make sure the building wouldn't collapse under the weight of alcohol. Visitors rafted across the punch before having a drink and toying with the remote control garnishes.

INDEX

SUPPLIERS

BLACK LIGHTS/ UV LIGHTS

You can buy a black light and fittings at any decent-sized hardware store or home renovation retail outlet. If you want something with a bit more punch, try a special effects supplier for a UV cannon. We use Stage Electrics, a special effects treasure trove that also supplies theatrical blood and an artificial snow machine.

FRUIT

If you are going to make a large amount of fruit jelly, it is worthwhile hitting up a wholesale market. Here in London we get up ridiculously early to catch the wholesale fruit and vegetable market at Borough Market. One pleasure of going this early is the local pub, which has a special market license. Because many of the traders will have been working all through the night, the pub is allowed to serve alcohol between 6 and 8.30 a.m.! In the US we suggest going to your local farmers' market for the best produce.

GELATIN

Gelatin can be found in the baking section of any half-decent supermarket (in the UK). Buy the fine leaf gelatin: Dr. Oetker's gelatin is what we use the most. Otherwise buy it online at www.oetkeronline.co.uk

GOLD

You could go to an art supply store for your gold. We don't. Ours is from Leyland, the builders' merchant, because it's cheaper. Further discounts are contingent on which soccer team you support. Make sure you buy gold over 22 karat so it is safe to eat. You can also order gold leaf online at www.cheftools.com.

TIKI

Cheeky Tiki (www.cheekytiki.com) is the best place for Samoan war staffs and dried puffer fish. Bamboo can be found at your nearest garden center.

BIBLIOGRAPHY

Archbold, Rick et al. *Last Dinner on the Titanic: Menus and Recipes from the Legendary Liner.* Toronto: Madison Press Books, 1997.

Beauman, Fran. *The Pineapple: King of Fruits.* London: Vintage, 2006.

Beeton, Isabella. *Book of Household Management.* Lewes: Southover Press, 2003.

Blumenthal, Heston. *The Big Fat Duck Cookbook.* London: Bloomsbury, 2008.

Brears, Peter. "Transparent Pleasures – The Story of the Jelly: Part One," in *Petits Propos Culinaires 53.* London: Prospect Books, 1996.

Brears, Peter. "Transparent Pleasures – The Story of the Jelly: Part Two 1700–1820, " in *Petits Propos Culinaires 54.* London: Prospect Books, 1996.

Brillat-Savarin, Jean. *The Physiology of Taste. New York*: Alfred A. Knopf, 1971.

Chambers, Anne. *The Practical Guide to Marbling Paper.* London: Thames and Hudson, 1992.

Cowen, Ruth. *Relish.* London: Weidenfeld & Nicolson, 2006.

Davies, Jennifer. *The Victorian Kitchen.* London: BBC Books, 1989.

Dawson, Thomas. *The Good Huswifes Jewell.* Amsterdam: Theatrum Orbis Terrarum, 1977.

Edwards, John (et al.) "The influence of eating location on the acceptability of identically prepared foods." *Journal of Food Quality and Preference* 14 (8) (2002): pp 647–652.

Fernandez-Armesto. *Food: a History.* London: Macmillan, 2001.

Fitzgerald, Robert. *Rowntree and the Marketing Revolution 1862–1969.* Cambridge: Cambridge University Press, 1995.

Harris, Henry G. and S.P. Borella. *All About Ices, Jellies and Creams.* London: Kegan Paul, 2002.

Henderson, Fergus. *Nose to Tail Eating.* London: Macmillan, 1999.

Horwitz and Singley, eds. *Eating Architecture.* Massachusetts: Massachusetts Institute of Technology, 2004.

Huysmans, J.K. *Against Nature.* Translated by Robert Baldick. Harmondsworth: Penguin Books, 1976.

Kelly, Ian. *Cooking For Kings: The Life of Antonin Careme the First Celebrity Chef.* London: Short Books, 2003.

Marshall, Agnes B. *Mrs. A.B. Marshall's Larger Cookery Book of Extra Recipes.* London: Marshall's School of Cookery, 1897.

McGee, Harold. *McGee on Food & Cooking: an Encyclopedia of Kitchen Science, History and Culture.* London: Hodder and Stoughton, 2004.

Plat, Hugh. *Delightes for Ladies.* London: Crosby Lockwood, 1948.

Richardson, Tim. *Sweets.* London: Bantam, 2002.

Rutherford, Jessica. *A Prince's Passion: the Life of the Royal Pavillion.* Brighton: Brighton and Hove City Council, 2003.

Shopsin, Kenny. E*at Me: The Food and Philosophy of Kenny Shopsin.* New York. Knopf, 2008.

Steingarten, Jeffrey. *It Must've Been Something I Ate.* New York: Vintage Books, 2003.

Strong, Roy. *Feast: a History of Grand Eating.* London: Jonathan Cape, 2002.

Taillevent. *Le Viendier de Taillevent.* Translated by James Prescott. Oregon: Alfarhaugr Publishing Society, 1989.

Taillevent. *The Cookery Book.* Translated by David Atkinson. York: Michael Sessions & Colleagues, 1992.

Theodore Garrett. *The Encyclopaedia of Practical Cookery.* London: Upcott Gill, 1892.

Toulmin Smith, Lucy, ed. *Expeditions to Prussia and the Holy Land made by Henry, Earl of Derby.* London: Camden Society, 1894.

Wilson, C. Anne. *Food and Drink in Britain: from the Stone Age to Recent Times.* London: Constable, 1973.

Young, Carolin. *Apples of Gold in Settings of Silver.* New York: Simon & Schuster, 2002.

Websites: Day, Ivan. www.historicfood.com

AUTHORS' ACKNOWLEDGMENTS

There's a vast crew of people who have helped us realize the jelly dream. Parents and families who took us seriously when we turned our backs on reasonable careers to become jellymongers. They've been first to be drafted in for madcap projects, schemes and scenarios and give the business a righteous backbone. To Abra Bompas, who put up with sticky floors when we started the business in her kitchen.

Our agent the mighty Isabel Atherton of Creative Authors who originated the concept of a jelly cookbook and has been heroic in making it reality.

Thanks to all the Anova Books people starting with our editor Emily Preece-Morrison, Polly Powell and Georgie Hewitt for hours of work and belief in this project. To photographer Chris Terry and stylist Wei Tang for making the recipes in the book look genius. To Mo Coppoletta and Hudson at New River Head, Jane and Mike at The Quality Chop House and Fontaine at Factory Studio for assistance with shoot locations. To Tamzin Ferdinando and Karl Blackwell for shoot assistance. And to Caroline Curtis and Constance Novis for editorial assistance.

To Greta Ilieva for taking the magical photograph of St. Paul's that has starred in newspapers on seven continents.

To Ivan Day, a major influence, inspiration and our food idol.

University College London and the Bartlett School of Architecture for generously lending us buildings, workshops and equipment. To Professor Stephen Gage for first encouraging us to explore the link between food and architecture through jelly, Dr. Andrea Sella for opening the doors of perception and his chemistry laboratory and Dr. James Kneale for the historical grounding.

A big shout-out to our talented crew and co-conspirators. The indomitable Robin Fegen, who has jellied all over the world while writing his book *Tracksuit: A Story About Pets 'n' Vets*. To Andrew Compton, Douglas Murphy, Nick Westby and Hugo

Richardson, a real vet. And not forgetting the scads of interns who produce the most astonishing results on ridiculously small budgets.

Elephant loads of thanks to everyone who got sucked into the process and who we've forgotten to thank here.

To Harry's girlfriend Cecilia Carey for spectacular stage design. To Sam's girlfriend, illustrator Emma Rios who gave us our first logo within a week of setting up and who forced us to get naked for her 2D banquet photograph — another photo that has gone around the world. They help at every event; apparently it's the only way to get to see their boyfriends. We'll go on holiday next year! With love…